QUILT-LOVERS' FAVORITES™

FROM AMERICAN PATCHWORK & QUILTING®

Better Homes and Gardens® Creative Collection™
Des Moines, Iowa

VOLUME 4

Better Homes and Gardens®

QUILT-LOVERS' FAVORITES™

FROM AMERICAN PATCHWORK & QUILTING®

Director of Editorial Administration	MICHAEL L. MAINE
Editor-in-Chief	BEVERLY RIVERS
Executive Editor	HEIDI KAISAND
Art Director	MELISSA GANSEN BEAUCHAMP
Senior Editor	JENNIFER ERBE KELTNER
Editors	MARY HELEN SCHILTZ AND DIANE YANNEY
Graphic Designer	MARY-BETH MAJEWSKI
Editorial Assistant	MARY IRISH
Contributing Editors	SUE BAHR AND SANDRA NEFF
Contributing Graphic Designer	BARBARA J. GORDON
Contributing Copy Editors	DIANE DORO, LISA FLYR, ANGELA INGLE, AND JENNIFER SPEER RAMUNDT
Quilt Tester	LAURA BOEHNKE
Technical Editor	LILA SCOTT
Contributing Watercolor Illustrator	ANN WEISS
Contributing Technical Illustrator	BARBARA J. GORDON
Publisher	STEVE LEVINSON
Consumer Products Associate Marketing Director	STEVE SWANSON
Business Director	CHRISTY LIGHT
Production Director	DOUGLAS M. JOHNSTON
Book Production Managers	PAM KVITNE AND MARJORIE J. SCHENKELBERG
Vice President Publishing Director	WILLIAM R. REED

Meredith
CORPORATION

Chairman and CEO	WILLIAM T. KERR
In Memoriam	E.T. MEREDITH III (1933-2003)

Meredith Publishing Group
President	STEPHEN M. LACY
Magazine Group President	JACK GRIFFIN
Creative Services	ELLEN DE LATHOUDER
Manufacturing	BRUCE HESTON
Consumer Marketing	KARLA JEFFRIES
Finance and Administration	MAX RUNCIMAN

Member HÎA
www.i-craft.com

Crafts.
Discover life's little
pleasures.

Audit Bureau of Circulations
Member

For book editorial questions, write:
Better Homes and Gardens Quilt-Lovers' Favorites • 1716 Locust St., Des Moines, IA 50309-3023

TREASURED QUILTS

Those who love to make quilts continually search for creative inspiration. We produced this fourth volume of Quilt-Lovers' Favorites™ to meet that need, pulling its 15 main projects directly from the pages of American Patchwork & Quilting® magazine. It wasn't hard to determine which projects should be included; they're the ones more often requested by readers and the ones most frequently submitted to our "From Our Readers" section.

As always, our hallmarks—full-size patterns and step-by-step instructions—accompany beautiful photographs of the finished quilts, but we didn't stop there. We have created new projects using blocks, units, or appliqué patterns found in the original quilts and offer color options wherever possible. Optional size charts mean you can alter quilt dimensions quickly and easily, and Quilter's Schoolhouse offers a start-to-finish reference guide on quiltmaking.

In these pages you'll find projects to enhance your decor, to give to family and friends, and to wear, frame, or take along on the road. We hope you enjoy this collection of quilts. You already know they're the Quilt-Lovers' Favorites.

Heidi Kaisand

Executive Editor, American Patchwork & Quilting®

TABLE *of* CONTENTS

4

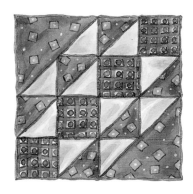

TIMELESS
TREASURES

Lovingly stitched, these vintage quilts have been enjoyed by generations. Their simple designs can be remade in endless ways. Re-create the late-18th-century "Oriole Circle" in reproduction prints, replace the two colors of "Twirling Patchwork" with a variety of hues, or try the early-19th-century "Steps to the Altar" in contemporary fabrics to make future heirloom quilts all your own.

ORIOLE *Circle*

Frieda Holt, a collector of antique quilts, found this late 1800s quilt at the bottom of a bargain bin. The quiltmaker used numerous fabric scraps to compose the individual blocks but assembled them with a single green print.

Materials

1¼ yards total of assorted dark red prints
   for blocks

2¼ yards total of assorted white shirting prints
   for blocks

2⅞ yards total of assorted brown prints for
   blocks and binding

3⅜ yards of green print for setting squares, setting
   triangles, and border

½ yard of white-and-red print for border

5¼ yards of backing fabric

76×93" of quilt batting

Finished quilt top: 70×86⅛"
Finished block: 11" square

Quantities specified for 44/45"-wide, 100% cotton fabrics. All measurements include a ¼" seam allowance. Sew with right sides together unless otherwise stated.

Cut the Fabrics

To make the best use of your fabrics, cut the pieces in the order that follows. The patterns are on *Pattern Sheet 1*. To make templates of patterns B and C, follow the instructions in Quilter's Schoolhouse, which begins on *page 150*.

From assorted dark red prints, cut:
- 400—1½×2½" rectangles

From assorted white shirting prints, cut:
- 18—1½×42" strips
- 480—1½×2½" rectangles

From assorted brown prints, cut:
- 8—2½×42" binding strips
- 9—1½×42" strips
- 20—3½" squares
- 80 *each* of patterns B and C

continued

From green print, cut:
- 4—4½×42" strips for border
- 5—2½×42" strips for border
- 4—16¾" squares, cutting each diagonally twice in an X for a total of 16 setting triangles (you'll have 2 leftover triangles)
- 12—11½" setting squares
- 2—8¾" squares, cutting each in half diagonally for a total of 4 corner triangles

From white-and-red print, cut:
- 5—2¼×42" strips for border

Make the Foundation Papers

1. With a pencil, trace Pattern A onto tracing paper 10 times. Transfer all lines and numbers and leave at least 2" between tracings. Cut out tracings. Place each tracing on top of a stack of seven unmarked sheets of tracing paper. (Freezer paper and typing paper also will work.) Staple each stack together.

2. Using a sewing machine with an unthreaded small-gauge needle set on 10 to 12 stitches per inch, sew precisely on all traced lines except the outer edges, stitching through all layers of paper.

3. Cut out each foundation paper on the outer traced lines to make a total of 80 foundation papers.

Assemble the Arcs

1. Place a white shirting print 1½×2½" rectangle atop a dark red print 1½×2½" rectangle. Put a foundation paper on top of the shirting rectangle (see Photo 1, *below*). Position layered rectangles under the foundation paper so their right edges are a scant ¼" beyond the first stitching line and about ⅜" above the top of the arc. With the foundation paper on top, sew on stitching line No. 1.

    Note: For photographic purposes, we used black thread to stitch these sample pieces. When you sew, we recommend using gray or a color that matches your fabric.

2. Press the dark red rectangle open from the fabric side (see Photo 2, *below*), pressing the seam allowance toward the dark red rectangle.

3. Trim the dark red rectangle to about ¼" beyond the next stitching line; trim both rectangles even with the top and bottom edges of the foundation paper (see Photo 3, *below*).

4. Position a second white shirting print rectangle under the trimmed dark red piece with the right edge ¼" beyond the second stitching line. Sew on stitching line No. 2 (see Photo 4, *below*).

5. Press the white rectangle open as before (see Photo 5, *opposite*), pressing the seam allowance toward the white rectangle. Trim the white rectangle to about ¼" beyond the next stitching line and even with the top and bottom edges of the foundation paper.

6. Continue adding rectangles, alternating fabrics and trimming as before, until you've pieced the entire arc (see Photo 6, top arc, *opposite*). With the blunt edge of a seam ripper, remove the tracing paper to make a pieced arc (see Photo 6, bottom arc, *opposite*).

7. Repeat steps 1 through 6 to make a total of 80 pieced arcs.

Assemble the Arc Units

1. Pin the center top of a pieced arc to the center top of a brown print C piece (marked with a • on the pattern). Then pin each arc end. Pin generously between the ends and the center (see Photo 7, *opposite*), using slender pins and picking up only a few threads at each position to achieve a smooth curve.

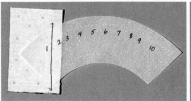

Photo 1

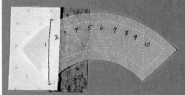

Photo 2

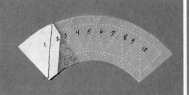

Photo 3

Photo 4

2. Sew together the pieces; to ensure sharp points, you may need to stitch a little to the right of the sewing line. You may stitch the pieces either by hand or machine. Hand stitching allows you to check for a smooth seam as you stitch because you can turn the piece over occasionally to look at the back. If you choose to machine-stitch, have the pieced arc on top when you put the pieces under the presser foot. Work slowly, stop the machine often with the needle down, and adjust the direction you're sewing as needed.

Press the seam allowance toward the brown print C piece.

3. In the same manner, add a brown print B piece to the bottom of the pieced arc to make an arc unit (see Photo 8, *below*). Press the seam allowance toward the brown print B piece. The pieced arc unit should measure 4½" square, including the seam allowances.

4. Repeat steps 1 through 3 to make a total of 80 pieced arc units.

Assemble the Blocks

I. Aligning long edges, sew two white shirting print 1½×42" strips to a brown print 1½×42" strip to make a strip set (see Diagram 1). Press the seam allowances toward the brown strip. Repeat to make a total of nine strip sets.

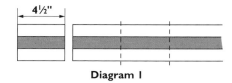

Diagram I

2. Cut the strip sets into eighty 4½"-wide segments.

3. Referring to Diagram 2 for placement, lay out four arc units, four white-and-brown 4½"-wide segments, and one brown print 3½" square in three horizontal rows.

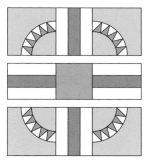

Diagram 2

4. Sew together the pieces in each row. Press the seam allowances toward the white-and-brown segments in each row. Then join the rows to make a block. Press the seam allowances in one direction. The pieced block should measure 11½" square, including the seam allowances.

5. Repeat steps 3 and 4 to make a total of 20 blocks.

Assemble the Quilt Center

I. Referring to the Quilt Assembly Diagram on *page 12*, lay out the 20 blocks, the 12 green print 11½" setting squares, and 14 green print setting triangles in diagonal rows.

2. Sew together the pieces in each diagonal row. Press the seam allowances toward the setting squares and triangles.

3. Join the rows. Press the seam allowances in one direction. Add the green print corner triangles to complete the quilt center. The quilt center should measure 63×78⅝", including the seam allowances.

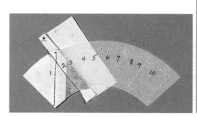

Photo 5

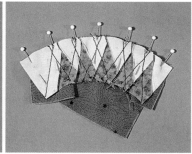

Photo 6

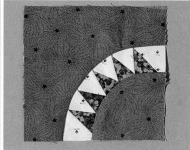

Photo 7

Photo 8

continued

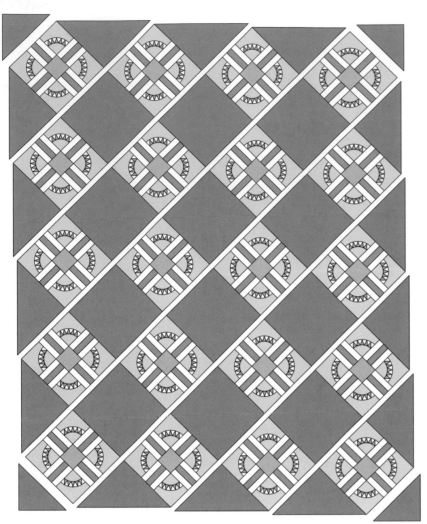

Quilt Assembly Diagram

Add the Borders

Note: The white-and-red print border is sewn only to the side edges of the quilt center.

1. Cut and piece the green print 4½×42" strips to make the following:
   • 2—4½×63" border strips

2. Sew the green print border strips to the top and bottom edges of the quilt center. Press the seam allowances toward the green print border.

3. Cut and piece the white-and-red print 2¼×42" strips to make the following:
   • 2—2¼×86⅝" border strips

4. Join the white-and-red print border strips to the side edges of the quilt center. Press the seam allowances toward the white-and-red print border.

5. Cut and piece the green print 2½×42" strips to make the following:
   • 2—2½×86⅝" border strips

6. Join the green print border strips to the side edges of the quilt center to complete the quilt top. Press the seam allowances toward the green print border.

Oriole Circle Quilt
optional sizes

If you'd like to make this quilt in a size other than for a twin bed, use the information *below*.

Alternate quilt sizes	Crib/Lap	Full/Queen	King
Number of blocks	12	30	36
Number of blocks wide by long	3×4	5×6	6×6
Number of setting squares	6	20	25
Finished size	54⅜×70½"	85⅝×101¾"	101¼×101¾"
Yardage requirements			
Assorted dark red prints	⅔ yard	1⅔ yards	2 yards
Assorted white shirting prints	1⅜ yards	3⅛ yards	3⅝ yards
Assorted brown prints	2 yards	4⅛ yards	4⅞ yards
Green print	2⅝ yards	5 yards	5⅞ yards
White-and-red print	⅓ yard	½ yard	½ yard
Backing	3½ yards	7⅔ yards	9 yards
Batting	61×77"	92×108"	108" square

Complete the Quilt

1. Layer the quilt top, batting, and backing according to the instructions in Quilter's Schoolhouse, which begins on *page 150*.

2. Quilt as desired. Hand-stitched diagonal lines crisscross on this antique quilt to accent it with diamond shapes.

3. Use the brown print 2½×42" strips to bind the quilt according to the instructions in Quilter's Schoolhouse.

SPRING QUILT

Bursting with color, this quilt sends rays of sunshine from fussy-cut hydrangeas.

Materials

¹⁄₃ yard of yellow print for blocks

¼ yard of blue print for blocks

¹⁄₈ yard of yellow plaid for blocks

¼ yard of small floral print for blocks

½ yard of large floral print for blocks and outer border

¼ yard of light blue print for blocks

⁵⁄₈ yard of dark blue print for blocks, inner border, and binding

1 yard of backing fabric

36" square of quilt batting

Finished quilt top: 31" square

Cut the Fabrics

To make the best use of your fabrics, cut the pieces in the order that follows. This project uses "Oriole Circle" patterns, which are on *Pattern Sheet 1*. To

make templates of patterns B and C, follow the instructions in Quilter's Schoolhouse, which begins on *page 150*.

Refer to Make the Foundation Papers on *page 10* to make a total of 16 perforated foundation papers.

From yellow print, cut:
* 96—1½×2½" rectangles

From blue print, cut:
* 80—1½×2½" rectangles

From yellow plaid, cut:
* 16 of Pattern B

From small floral print, cut:
* 16 of Pattern C

From large floral print, cut:
* 4—4×33½" outer border strips
* 4—3½" squares, being sure to fussy-cut desired pattern

From light blue print, cut:
* 4—1½×42" strips

continued

From dark blue print, cut:
- 4—2½×42" binding strips
- 2—1½×42" strips
- 4—1½×26½" inner border strips

Assemble the Arc Units

1. Referring to Assemble the Arcs on *page 10*, use the yellow print rectangles and blue print rectangles to make a total of 16 pieced arcs.

2. Referring to Assemble the Arc Units on *page 10*, add a yellow plaid B piece and a small floral print C piece to each pieced arc to make a total of 16 pieced arc units. Each pieced arc unit should measure 4½" square, including the seam allowances.

Assemble the Blocks

1. Referring to Assemble the Blocks on *page 11*, use two light blue print 1½×42" strips and one dark blue print 1½×42" strip to make a strip set.

2. Repeat to make a second strip set, cutting the strip sets into sixteen 4½"-wide segments.

3. Use the segments, arc units, and large floral print 3½" squares to make a total of four blocks.

Assemble the Quilt Center

1. Referring to the photograph on *page 13* for placement, lay out the four pieced blocks in pairs. Sew together the pairs. Press the seam allowances in opposite directions.

2. Join the pairs to make the quilt center. Press the seam allowance in one direction. The pieced quilt center should measure 22½" square, including the seam allowances.

Add the Borders

1. With midpoints aligned, sew the dark blue print 1½×26½" inner border strips to opposite edges of the quilt center, beginning and ending the seams ¼" from the corners. Add the remaining dark blue print 1½×26½" inner border strips to the remaining edges of the quilt center, mitering the corners. For information on mitering corners, see the Mitered Border Corner instructions in Quilter's Schoolhouse, which begins on *page 150*. Press all seam allowances toward the inner border.

2. As in Step 1, sew the large floral print 4×33½" outer border strips to the quilt center edges, mitering the corners. Press all seam allowances toward the inner border.

Complete the Quilt

1. Layer the quilt top, batting, and backing according to the instructions in Quilter's Schoolhouse, which begins on *page 150*. Quilt as desired.

2. Use the dark blue print 2½×42" strips to bind the quilt according to the instructions in Quilter's Schoolhouse.

FRAMED BLOCK

Black-and-white fabrics turn a traditional

block into a contemporary work of art.

Materials

Scraps of assorted black prints

⅛ yard *each* of white print and gray print

¼ yard of black-and-white print

⅛ yard of black-and-white stripe

Mat and frame

Cut the Fabrics

To make the best use of your fabrics, cut the pieces in the order that follows. This project uses "Oriole Circle" patterns, which are on *Pattern Sheet 1*. To make templates of patterns B and C, follow the instructions in Quilter's Schoolhouse, which begins on *page 150*.

Refer to Make the Foundation Papers on *page 10* to make a total of four perforated foundation papers.

From assorted black prints, cut:
- 20—1½×2½" rectangles

From white print, cut:
- 24—1½×2½" rectangles

From gray print, cut:
- 2—1½×20" strips
- 1—1½×3½" strip

From black-and-white print, cut:
- 4 *each* of patterns B and C

From black-and-white stripe, cut:
- 1—1½×20" strip
- 2—1½×3½" strips

Assemble the Arc Units

1. Referring to Assemble the Arcs on *page 10*, use the black print rectangles and white print rectangles to make a total of four pieced arcs.

2. Referring to Assemble the Arc Units on *page 10*, add black-and-white print B and C pieces to each pieced arc to make a total of four arc units. Each pieced arc unit should measure 4½" square, including the seam allowances.

Assemble the Block

1. Referring to Assemble the Blocks on *page 11*, steps 1 and 2, use the two gray print 1½×20" strips and the black-and-white stripe 1½×20" strip to make a strip set. Cut the strip set into four 4½"-wide segments and one 1½"-wide segment (see Diagram 1).

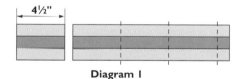

Diagram 1

2. Aligning long edges, sew the two black-and-white stripe 1½×3½" strips to the gray 1½×3½" strip to make a strip set. Press the seam allowances toward the black-and-white stripe strips. Cut the strip set into two 1½"-wide segments (see Diagram 2).

Diagram 2

3. Referring to Diagram 3, sew together the three 1½"-wide segments to make a Nine-Patch unit. Press the seam allowances toward the center segment. The Nine-Patch unit should measure 3½" square, including the seam allowances.

Diagram 3

4. Referring to Diagram 4 for placement, lay out the four arc units, the four 4½"-wide segments, and the Nine-Patch unit in three horizontal rows.

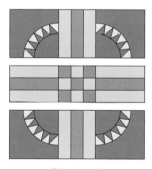

Diagram 4

5. Sew together the pieces in each row. Press the seam allowances toward the 4½"-wide segments in each row.

6. Join the rows to make a block. Press the seam allowances in one direction. The pieced block should measure 11½" square, including the seam allowances.

Complete the Project

Frame as desired. Consider choosing an inner mat in a color that complements your decor.

Twirling *Patchwork*

The graphic elements of the block making up this antique quilt offer multiple layout possibilities. Experimenting with color placement and unit rotation, as quilt tester Laura Boehnke did on page 20, yields strikingly different results.

Materials

6⅞ yards of red print for blocks, border, and binding

5½ yards of muslin for blocks

6 yards of backing fabric

72×102" of quilt batting

Finished quilt top: 66×96"
Finished block: 10" square

Quantities specified for 44/45"-wide, 100% cotton fabrics. All measurements include a ¼" seam allowance. Sew with right sides together unless otherwise stated.

continued

Cut the Fabrics

To make the best use of your fabrics, cut the pieces in the order that follows. The patterns are on *Pattern Sheet 2*. To make templates of the patterns, follow the instructions in Quilter's Schoolhouse, which begins on *page 150*.

From red print, cut:
- 8—3½×42" strips for border
- 9—2½×42" binding strips
- 108—2⅞" squares, cutting each in half diagonally for a total of 216 triangles, *or* 216 of Pattern C
- 216 *each* of patterns A and B reversed

From muslin, cut:
- 108—2⅞" squares, cutting each in half diagonally for a total of 216 triangles, *or* 216 of Pattern C
- 216 *each* of patterns A reversed and B

Assemble the Blocks

1. Referring to Diagram 1 for placement, sew together one red print A piece, one muslin B piece, and one red print C triangle to make a Subunit 1. Press the seam allowances toward the red print pieces. Repeat to make a total of 216 of Subunit 1.

Diagram 1
Subunit 1

2. Referring to Diagram 2, sew together one muslin A reversed piece, one red print B reversed piece, and one muslin C triangle to make a Subunit 2. Press the seam allowances toward the red print piece. Repeat to make a total of 216 of Subunit 2.

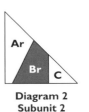

Diagram 2
Subunit 2

3. Sew together one Subunit 1 and one Subunit 2 to make a Quarter unit (see Diagram 3). Press the seam allowance to one side. The pieced Quarter unit should measure 5½" square, including the seam allowances. Repeat to make a total of 216 Quarter units.

Diagram 3
Quarter unit

4. Referring to Diagram 4, *opposite*, for placement, lay out four Quarter units in pairs. Sew together the units in pairs. Press the seam allowances in opposite directions. Then join the pairs to make a

block. Press the seam allowance in one direction. The pieced block should measure 10½" square, including the seam allowances. Repeat to make a total of 54 blocks.

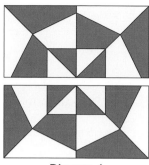

Diagram 4

Assemble the Quilt Center

1. Referring to the photograph *opposite* for placement, lay out the 54 blocks in nine horizontal rows.

2. Sew together the blocks in each row. Press the seam allowances in each row in one direction, alternating the direction with each row.

3. Join the rows to complete the quilt center. Press the seam allowances in one direction. The pieced quilt center should measure 60½×90½", including the seam allowances.

Add the Border

1. Cut and piece the red print 3½×42" strips to make the following:
- 2—3½×96½" border strips
- 2—3½×60½" border strips

2. Sew the short border strips to the top and bottom edges of the pieced quilt center. Then add the long border strips to the side edges of the pieced quilt center to complete the quilt top. Press all seam allowances toward the red print border.

Complete the Quilt

1. Layer the quilt top, batting, and backing according to the instructions in Quilter's Schoolhouse, which begins on *page 150.*

2. Quilt as desired. This antique quilt was hand-quilted ¼" inside the edges of each piece.

3. Use the red print 2½×42" strips to bind the quilt according to the instructions in Quilter's Schoolhouse.

Twirling Patchwork Quilt
optional sizes

If you'd like to make this quilt in a size other than for a twin bed, use the information *below.*

Alternate quilt sizes	Crib	Lap	Full/Queen	King
Number of blocks	12	20	72	100
Number of blocks wide by long	3×4	4×5	8×9	10×10
Finished size	36×46"	46×56"	86×96"	106" square
Yardage requirements				
Red print	2¼ yards	3¼ yards	8⅜ yards	11⅓ yards
Muslin	1⅜ yards	2¼ yards	6⅞ yards	9½ yards
Backing	1½ yards	2⅝ yards	7⅔ yards	9⅓ yards
Batting	42×52"	52×62"	92×102"	112" square

continued

optional colors

"This is one of those patterns with two different designs going on at the same time," quilt tester Laura Boehnke says. "Color placement really brings out those two designs in different ways."

Contrast also plays an important part in the overall appearance of these quilts. The use of light, medium, and dark fabrics clarifies the shapes that emerge, whether they are circles, pinwheels, or stars. The shapes take on greater dimensions when the fabrics have more contrast.

Through color placement and the selection of fabrics with lots of contrast, Laura was able to accentuate either the pinwheel or the four-pointed star (see also Batik Quilt, *pages 21–22*).

Option 1

Light and dark fabrics are placed to bring out the pattern's circles. Low-contrast hues create subtle pinwheels or four-pointed stars between the circles.

Option 2

Using different prints of the same color, such as three greens or three blues, defines each of the blocks and its center pinwheel. Four-color stars emerge where the blocks intersect. The contrasting yellow background assures an overall continuity.

Option 3

Light-color conversational prints make the small red pinwheels and large blue stars pop. The use of high contrast fabrics and their placement are key to this design. Extend the quilt top's color palette into the border for more action.

BATIK QUILT

This quilt radiates faceted stars, with two different prints making up each star.

Materials

½ yard of green plaid for blocks and inner border

9—6×24" pieces of assorted gold batiks for blocks

9—6×24" pieces of assorted orange batiks for blocks

9—9×22" pieces (fat eighths) of assorted green batiks for blocks

⅞ yard of dark green batik for outer border and binding

1¼ yards of backing fabric

43" of quilt batting

Finished quilt top: 37" square

Cut the Fabrics

To make the best use of your fabrics, cut the pieces in the order that follows. This project uses "Twirling Patchwork" patterns, which are on *Pattern Sheet 2*. To make templates of the patterns, follow the instructions in Quilter's Schoolhouse, which begins on *page 150*.

From green plaid, cut:
- 2—1½×32½" inner border strips
- 2—1½×30½" inner border strips
- 18—2⅞" squares, cutting each in half diagonally for a total of 36 triangles, *or* 36 of Pattern C

From *each* gold batik, cut:
- 4 of Pattern A

From *each* orange batik, cut:
- 4 of Pattern A reversed

From *each* green batik, cut:
- 4 *each* of patterns B and B reversed

From dark green batik, cut:
- 4—2½×42" binding strips
- 2—3×37½" outer border strips
- 2—3×32½" outer border strips

- 18—2⅞" squares, cutting each in half diagonally for a total of 36 triangles, *or* 36 of Pattern C

Assemble the Blocks

Referring to the photograph on *page 22* for placement and Assemble the Blocks on *page 18*, use four matching gold batik A pieces, four matching orange batik A reversed pieces, eight matching green batik B and B reversed pieces, four green plaid C triangles, and four dark green C triangles to make a block. Repeat to make a total of nine blocks.

Assemble the Quilt Center

1. Lay out the nine blocks in three rows. Sew together the blocks in each row. Press the seam allowances in each row in one direction, alternating the direction with each row.

2. Join the rows to make the quilt center. Press the seam allowances in one direction. The pieced quilt center should measure 30½" square, including the seam allowances.

Add the Borders

1. Sew the green plaid 1½×30½" inner border strips to opposite edges of the quilt center. Add the

continued

green plaid 1½×32½" inner border strips to the remaining edges of the quilt center. Press the seam allowances toward the inner border.

2. Sew the dark green batik 3×32½" outer border strips to opposite edges of the quilt center. Then join the dark green batik 3×37½" outer border strips to the remaining edges of the quilt center to complete the quilt top. Press all seam allowances toward the outer border.

Complete the Quilt
1. Layer the quilt top, batting, and backing according to the instructions in Quilter's Schoolhouse, which begins on *page 150*. Quilt as desired.

2. Use the dark green batik 2½×42" strips to bind the quilt according to the instructions in Quilter's Schoolhouse.

FLOOR PILLOW

Fun prints in pastel colors make this 27-inch floor pillow a wonderful gift you can complete in a weekend.

Materials

¼ yard *each* of assorted pastel green, blue, and lavender prints for blocks, border, and binding

½ yard of white-and-blue print for blocks

1⅝ yards of white-and-lavender print for border and backing

33" square of muslin for lining

33" square of quilt batting

27"-square pillow form

Finished pillow cover: 27" square

Cut the Fabrics
To make the best use of your fabrics, cut the pieces in the order that follows. This project uses "Twirling Patchwork" patterns, which are on *Pattern Sheet 2*. To make templates, follow the instructions in Quilter's Schoolhouse, which begins on *page 150*.

From assorted pastel green, blue, and lavender prints, cut:
- 3—2½×42" binding strips (from same print)
- 16 *each* of patterns A and B reversed (8 sets of 4)
- 4—4" squares (1 set of 4)
- 8—2⅞" squares, cutting each in half diagonally for a total of 16 triangles, *or* 16 of Pattern C (4 sets of 4)

From white-and-blue print, cut:
- 16 *each* of patterns A reversed and B
- 8—2⅞" squares, cutting each in half diagonally for a total of 16 triangles, *or* 16 of Pattern C

From white-and-lavender print, cut:
- 2—22½×27½" rectangles
- 4—4×20½" strips for border

Assemble the Blocks
Referring to the photograph *opposite* and Assemble the Blocks on *page 18*, use the assorted green, blue, lavender, and the white-and-blue print A, B, and C pieces to make a block. *Note:* Each block contains four prints. Repeat to make a total of four blocks.

Assemble the Pillow Center

1. Referring to the photograph *above* for placement, lay out the four blocks in pairs. Sew together the pairs. Press the seam allowances in opposite directions.

2. Join the pairs to make the pillow center. Press the seam allowance in one direction. The pieced pillow center should measure 20½" square, including the seam allowances.

Add the Border

1. Sew a white-and-lavender print 4×20½" border strip to opposite edges of the pieced pillow center. Press the seam allowances toward the white-and-lavender print border.

2. Sew an assorted pastel print 4" square to each end of the remaining white-and-lavender print 4×20½" border strips to make two pieced border units. Press the seam allowances toward the white-and-lavender print strips. Join the pieced border units to the remaining edges of the pieced pillow center to complete the pillow

top. Press the seam allowances toward the white-and-lavender print border.

Complete the Pillow

1. Layer the pillow top, batting, and the muslin lining; baste the layers. Quilt as desired. Trim the excess batting and muslin lining even with the raw edges of the pillow top.

2. Fold and press under ¼" along a long edge of each white-and-lavender print 22½×27½" rectangle. Press under an additional 3" along the same edge; topstitch. Overlap the two pieces to form a 27" square for the pillow back.

3. With wrong sides together, layer the pillow back and the pillow top; baste the layers together, sewing a scant ¼" from the raw edges.

4. Use the pastel print 2½×42" strips to bind the pillow top and back according to the instructions in Quilter's Schoolhouse, beginning on *page 150*.

5. Insert the pillow form through the back opening.

STEPS TO THE *Altar*

The maker of this early-1900s quilt cut and pieced 3,445 squares by hand. A rotary cutter speeds the traditional method these days, and strip piecing makes it go even faster. Instructions for both methods follow.

Materials

1 yard of solid green for blocks and inner border

1¼ yards of solid orange for blocks and
middle border

2¼ yards of solid black for blocks,
outer border, and binding

60—⅛-yard pieces of assorted light and dark prints
for blocks and pieced border

5½ yards of backing fabric

82×97" of quilt batting

Finished quilt top: 75¼×90¼"
Finished block: 8¾" square

Quantities specified for 44/45"-wide, 100% cotton fabrics. All measurements include a ¼" seam allowance. Sew with right sides together unless otherwise stated.

Traditional Method
Cut the Fabrics

To make the best use of your fabrics, cut the pieces in the order that follows.

From solid green, cut:
- 8—2×42" strips for inner border
- 155—1¾" squares

From solid orange, cut:
- 8—2×42" strips for middle border
- 248—1¾" squares

From solid black, cut:
- 9—2½×42" binding strips
- 9—2×42" strips for outer border
- 372—1¾" squares

From *each* assorted print, cut:
- 45—1¾" squares (you'll cut a total of 2700 squares and have 30 leftover)

continued

Assemble Block A

1. Referring to Diagram 1 for placement, lay out the following 1¾" squares: five solid green, eight solid orange, 12 solid black, and 24 assorted prints in seven horizontal rows.

Diagram 1
Block A

2. Sew together the squares in each row. Press the seam allowances in one direction, alternating the direction with each row. Then join the rows to make a Block A. Press the seam allowances in one direction. Pieced Block A should measure 9¼" square, including the seam allowances.

3. Repeat steps 1 and 2 to make a total of 31 of Block A.

Assemble Block B

1. Referring to Diagram 2, lay out 49 assorted print 1¾" squares in seven horizontal rows.

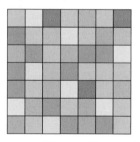

Diagram 2
Block B

2. Sew together the squares in each row. Press the seam allowances in one direction, alternating the direction with each row. Join the rows to make a Block B. Press the seam allowances in one direction. Pieced Block B should measure 9¼" square, including the seam allowances.

3. Repeat steps 1 and 2 to make a total of 32 of Block B.

Assemble the Quilt Center

1. Referring to the photograph on *page 28*, lay out the 63 pieced blocks in nine horizontal rows, alternating blocks A and B.

2. Sew together the blocks in each row. Press the seam allowances in one direction, alternating the direction with each row. Then join the rows to make the quilt center. Press the seam allowances in one direction. The quilt center should measure 61¾×79¼", including the seam allowances.

Add the Pieced Border

1. Sew together 49 assorted print 1¾" squares in a row to make the top pieced border strip. Press the seam allowances in one direction. Repeat to make the bottom pieced border strip. Join the pieced border strips to the top and bottom edges of the pieced quilt center. Press the seam allowances in one direction.

2. Sew together 65 assorted print 1¾" squares in a row to make a strip. Repeat to make a second strip. Press the strips' seam allowances in opposite directions. Sew the two pieced strips together to make a side pieced border unit. Repeat to make a second side pieced border unit. Join the pieced border units to the side edges of the pieced quilt center. Press the seam allowances in one direction. The quilt center should now measure 66¾×81¼", including the seam allowances.

Complete the Quilt

Refer to the instructions under Add the Remaining Borders and Complete the Quilt on *page 29* to finish the quilt.

Strip-Piecing Method
Cut the Fabrics

To make the best use of your fabrics, cut the pieces in the order that follows.

From solid green, cut:
- 8—2×42" strips for inner border
- 9—1¾×42" strips

From solid orange, cut:
- 8—2×42" strips for middle border
- 13—1¾×42" strips

From solid black, cut:
- 9—2½×42" binding strips
- 9—2×42" strips for outer border
- 19—1¾×42" strips

From *each* assorted print, cut:
- 2—1¾×42" strips

From assorted print scraps, cut:
- 8—1¾" squares

Assemble Block A

1. Referring to Diagram 3 for color placement, sew together six assorted print 1¾×42" strips and one solid black 1¾×42" strip to make a strip set. Press the seam allowances toward the center strip. Repeat to make a total of three strip sets.

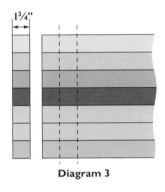

Diagram 3

2. Cut the strip sets into sixty-two 1¾"-wide segments.

3. Referring to Diagram 4, sew together four assorted print 1¾×42" strips, two solid black 1¾×42" strips, and one solid orange 1¾×42" strip to make a strip set. Press the seam allowances away from the center strip. Repeat to make a total of three strip sets.

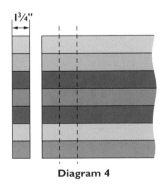

Diagram 4

4. Cut the strip sets into sixty-two 1¾"-wide segments.

5. Referring to Diagram 5, sew together two assorted print 1¾×42" strips, two solid black 1¾×42" strips, two solid orange 1¾×42" strips, and one solid green 1¾×42" strip to make a strip set. Press the seam allowances toward the center strip. Repeat to make a total of three strip sets.

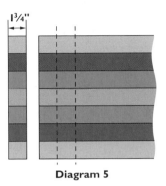

Diagram 5

6. Cut the strip sets into sixty-two 1¾"-wide segments.

7. Referring to Diagram 6, sew together two solid black 1¾×42" strips, two solid orange 1¾×42" strips, and three solid green 1¾×42" strips to make a strip set. Press the seam allowances away from the center strip. Repeat to make a total of two strip sets.

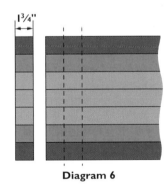

Diagram 6

8. Cut the strip sets into thirty-one 1¾"-wide segments.

9. Referring to Diagram 7 on *page 28*, lay out two Step 2 segments, two Step 4 segments, two Step 6 segments, and one Step 8 segment. Sew together the segments to make a Block A. Press the seam allowances in one direction. Pieced Block A should measure 9¼" square, including the seam allowances.

continued

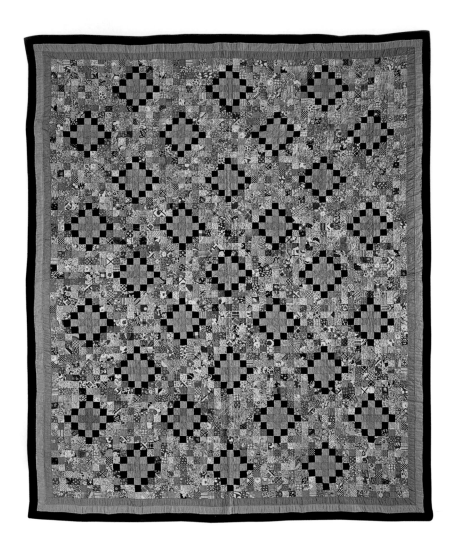

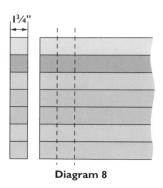

Diagram 8

2. Cut the strip sets into 1¾"-wide segments for a total of 274. Set aside 50 segments for the pieced border.

3. Referring to Diagram 9, lay out seven 1¾"-wide segments. Sew together the segments to make a Block B. Press the seam allowances in one direction. Pieced Block B should measure 9¼" square, including the seam allowances.

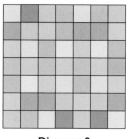

Diagram 9
Block B

4. Repeat Step 3 to make a total of 32 of Block B.

Assemble the Quilt Center

1. Referring to the photograph *left*, lay out the 63 pieced blocks in nine horizontal rows, alternating blocks A and B.

2. Sew together the blocks in each row. Press the seam allowances in one direction, alternating the direction with each row. Then join the rows to make the quilt center. Press the seam allowances in one direction. The pieced quilt center should measure 61¾×79¼", including the seam allowances.

Add the Pieced Border

1. Sew together in a row seven assorted print 1¾"-wide segments to make the top pieced border strip. Press the seam allowances in one

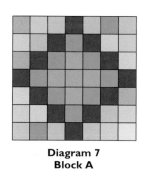

Diagram 7
Block A

10. Repeat Step 9 to make a total of 31 of Block A.

Assemble Block B

1. Referring to Diagram 8, sew together seven assorted print 1¾×42" strips to make a strip set. Repeat to make a total of 12 strip sets. Press the seam allowances in one direction in each strip set, alternating the direction with each set.

direction. Repeat to make the bottom pieced border strip. Join the pieced border strips to the top and bottom edges of the pieced quilt center. Press the seam allowances in one direction.

2. Sew together in a row nine assorted print 1¾"-wide segments to make a strip. Add two assorted print 1¾" squares to one end of the strip. Repeat to make a second strip. Press the seam allowances of the pieced strips in opposite directions. Sew the two pieced strips together to make a side border unit. Repeat to make a second side border unit. Join the side border units to the side edges of the pieced quilt center. Press the seam allowances in one direction. The pieced quilt center should now measure 66¾x81¾", including the seam allowances.

Add the Remaining Borders

1. Cut and piece the solid green 2x42" strips to make the following:
   - 2—2x84¾" inner border strips
   - 2—2x66¾" inner border strips

2. Sew the short inner border strips to the top and bottom edges of the pieced quilt center. Then add the long inner border strips to the side edges of the pieced quilt center. Press all seam allowances toward the solid green inner border.

3. Cut and piece the solid orange 2x42" strips to make the following:
   - 2—2x87¾" middle border strips
   - 2—2x69¾" middle border strips

4. Sew the short middle border strips to the top and bottom edges of the pieced quilt center. Then add the long middle border strips to the side edges of the pieced quilt center. Press all seam allowances toward the solid orange middle border.

5. Cut and piece the solid black 2x42" strips to make the following:
   - 2—2x90¾" outer border strips
   - 2—2x72¾" outer border strips

6. Sew the short outer border strips to the top and bottom edges of the pieced quilt center. Then add the long outer border strips to the side edges of the pieced quilt center to complete the quilt top. Press all seam allowances toward the solid black outer border.

Complete the Quilt

1. Layer the quilt top, batting, and backing according to the instructions in Quilter's Schoolhouse, which begins on *page 150*. Quilt as desired.

2. Use the solid black 2½x42" strips to bind the quilt according to the instructions in Quilter's Schoolhouse.

Steps to the Altar Quilt

optional sizes

If you'd like to make this quilt in a size other than for a twin bed, use the information *below.*

Alternate quilt sizes	Lap	Full/Queen	King
Number of Block A	17	40	60
Number of Block B	18	41	61
Number of blocks wide by long	5x7	9x9	11x11
Finished size	57¾x72¾"	92¾x90¼"	110¼x107¾"
Yardage requirements			
Solid green	¾ yard	1¼ yards	1½ yards
Solid orange	⅞ yard	1½ yards	1¾ yards
Solid black	1⅔ yards	2⅝ yards	3¼ yards
Assorted prints	3¼ yards	4½ yards	6 yards
Backing	3⅔ yards	8⅛ yards	9⅝ yards
Batting	64x79"	99x97"	117x114"

BABY QUILT

Yellow punches up the soft colors of peach,

green, and aqua in this easy-to-make,

two-block quilt.

Materials

¼ yard of yellow dot print for blocks

1⅛ yards of aqua dot print for blocks, inner border, and binding

¾ yard of peach dot print for blocks and outer border

2 yards total of assorted green, aqua, peach and yellow prints for blocks

3⅛ yards of backing fabric

56" square of quilt batting

Finished quilt top: 49¼" square

Cut the Fabrics

To make the best use of your fabrics, cut the pieces in the order that follows.

From yellow dot print, cut:
- 65—1¾" squares

From aqua dot print, cut:
- 5—2½×42" binding strips
- 5—2×42" strips for inner border
- 104—1¾" squares

From peach dot print, cut:
- 5—1¾×42" strips for outer border
- 156—1¾" squares

From assorted green, aqua, peach, and yellow prints, cut:
- 900—1¾" squares

Assemble Block A

Referring to the photograph *right* and Assemble Block A on *page 26*, use the following 1¾" squares to make a Block A: five yellow dot print, eight aqua dot print, 12 peach dot print, and 24 assorted green, aqua, peach, and yellow prints. Repeat to make a total of 13 of Block A.

Assemble Block B

Referring to the photograph *above right* and Assemble Block B on *page 26*, use 49 assorted green, aqua, peach, and yellow print 1¾" squares to make a Block B. Repeat to make a total of 12 of Block B.

Assemble the Quilt Center

1. Referring to the photograph *above right*, lay out the blocks in five horizontal rows, alternating blocks A and B.

2. Sew together the blocks in each row. Press the seam allowances in one direction, alternating the direction with each row. Then join the rows to make the quilt center. Press the seam allowances in one direction. The quilt center should measure 44¼" square, including the seam allowances.

Add the Borders

1. Cut and piece the aqua dot print 2×42" strips to make the following:
   - 2—2×47¼" inner border strips
   - 2—2×44¼" inner border strips

2. Sew the short inner border strips to opposite edges of the pieced quilt center. Then add the

long inner border strips to the remaining edges of the pieced quilt center. Press all seam allowances toward the aqua dot print inner border.

3. Cut and piece the peach dot print 1¾×42" strips to make the following:
   - 2—1¾×49¾" outer border strips
   - 2—1¾×47¼" outer border strips

4. Sew the short outer border strips to opposite edges of the pieced quilt center. Then add the long outer border strips to the remaining edges of the pieced quilt center to complete the quilt top. Press all seam allowances toward the aqua dot print inner border.

Complete the Quilt

1. Layer the quilt top, batting, and backing according to the instructions in Quilter's Schoolhouse, which begins on *page 150*. Quilt as desired.

2. Use the aqua dot print 2½×42" strips to bind the quilt according to the instructions in Quilter's Schoolhouse.

TABLE RUNNER

Combine holiday fabrics and gold lamé

to create this elegant table runner. For

summertime entertaining, choose red, white,

and blue fabrics for a patriotic look.

Materials

⅛ yard of gold print for blocks

⅛ yard of rose print for blocks and second border

¼ yard of green-and-gold print for blocks and
    fourth border

⅛ yard of dark green print for blocks and
    third border

¼ yard total of assorted green prints for blocks

⅓ yard of gold lamé for first border and binding

⅝ yard of backing fabric

21×39" of quilt batting

Gold metallic thread for quilting

Finished quilt top: 14¾×32¼"

Cut the Fabrics

To make the best use of your fabrics, cut the pieces in the order that follows.

From gold print, cut:
- 10—1¾" squares

From rose print, cut:
- 2—1×28¼" second border strips
- 2—1×9¾" second border strips
- 16—1¾" squares

From green-and-gold print, cut:
- 2—2×32¾" fourth border strips
- 2—2×12¼" fourth border strips
- 24—1¾" squares

From dark green print, cut:
- 2—1¼×29¾" third border strips
- 2—1¼×10¾" third border strips
- 24—1¾" squares

From assorted green prints, cut:
- 73—1¾" squares

From gold lamé, cut:
- 3—2½×42" binding strips
- 2—¾×27¼" first border strips
- 2—¾×9¼" first border strips

Assemble Block A

Referring to the photograph *above* and Assemble Block A on *page 26*, use the following 1¾" squares to make a Block A: five gold print, eight rose print, 12 green-and-gold print, 12 dark green print, and 12 assorted green prints. Repeat to make a second Block A.

Assemble Block B

Referring to the photograph *above* and Assemble Block B on *page 26*, use 49 assorted green print 1¾" squares to make a Block B.

Assemble the Quilt Center

Referring to the photograph *above,* lay out the three pieced blocks in a row with Block B in the center. Join the blocks to make the quilt center; press the seam allowances in one direction. The quilt center should measure 9¼×26¾", including the seam allowances.

Add the Borders

1. Sew the gold lamé ¾×9¼" first border strips to the short edges of the pieced quilt center. Then add the gold lamé ¾×27¼" first border

strips to the long edges of the pieced quilt center. Press all seam allowances toward the gold lamé border.

2. Sew the rose print 1×9¾" second border strips to the short edges of the quilt center. Then add the rose print 1×28¼" second border strips to the long edges of the quilt center. Press all seam allowances toward the rose print border.

3. Sew the dark green print 1¼×10¾" third border strips to the short edges of the quilt center. Then add the dark green print 1¼×29¾" third border strips to the long edges of the quilt center. Press all seam allowances toward the dark green print border.

4. Sew the green-and-gold print 2×12¼" fourth border strips to the short edges of the quilt center. Then add the green-and-gold print 2×32¾" fourth border strips to the long edges of the quilt center to complete the quilt top. Press all seam allowances toward the green-and-gold print border.

Complete the Quilt

1. Layer the quilt top, batting, and backing according to the instructions in Quilter's Schoolhouse, which begins on *page 150*. Quilt a crosshatch design with gold metallic thread.

2. Use the gold lamé 2½×42" strips to bind the quilt according to the instructions in Quilter's Schoolhouse.

ROW-BY-ROW
ATTRACTIONS

Quilters have long appreciated uncomplicated

projects—and row quilts fit that description.

Natural projects for several quilters to make as

a group, these quilts not only provide simplicity

of design but also variety. In "Twilight," the pieced

rows wrap around a center four-block unit;

"Sisters' Starberries" and "Texas Stars" combine

machine piecing and appliqué to create dynamic,

one-of-a-kind quilts.

Twilight

A collaborative effort between Leslie Beck and her staff at Fiber Mosaics resulted in this scrappy, medallion-style quilt. Leslie pulled together an assortment of colors and prints for this project, and if she ran out of one fabric, she just used something similar.

Materials

¾ yard of gold print for blocks

4 yards total of assorted light, medium, and
  dark prints for blocks and borders

1 yard of tan print No. 1 for blocks and outer border

1 yard of tan print No. 2 for blocks and outer border

1 yard of black star print for border and binding

3⅝ yards of backing fabric

65" square of quilt batting

Finished quilt top: 59" square
Finished Sunshine block: 9" square
Finished Friendship Star block: 4½" square
Finished Bear's Paw block: 4½" square
Finished Log Cabin block: 5×4½"
Finished Ohio Star block: 6" square

Quantities specified for 44/45"-wide, 100% cotton fabrics. All measurements include a ¼" seam allowance. Sew with right sides together unless otherwise stated.

About this Design

A series of borders surrounding a center unit give movement to this quilt top composed of five different blocks. The following instructions are atypical: Rather than working in sections, first you assemble all the individual blocks, then create the center unit, and finally assemble and add the borders.

Cut the Fabrics

To make the best use of your fabrics, cut the pieces in the order that follows. There are no pattern pieces for this quilt; the letter and number designations are for placement purposes only.

continued

Diagram 1

Diagram 2

2. Sew corner units to opposite edges of a gold print A square (see Diagram 2). Then join the remaining corner units to the remaining edges of the gold print A square to make a center unit. Press all seam allowances toward the gold print A square.

3. Sew together one gold print C triangle and one dark print C triangle to make a triangle-square (see Diagram 3). Press the seam allowance toward the dark print triangle. The triangle-square should measure 2" square, including the seam allowances. Repeat to make a total of eight triangle-squares.

Diagram 3

Diagram 4

4. Referring to Diagram 4, sew together a gold print D triangle and two dark print C triangles to make a Flying Geese unit. Press the seam allowances toward the dark print C triangles. The pieced Flying Geese unit should measure 2×3½", including the seam allowances. Repeat to make a total of four Flying Geese units.

Assemble the Blocks
Sunshine Blocks
The cutting and assembly instructions that follow are for making one Sunshine block. Repeat to make a total of eight Sunshine blocks.

From gold print, cut:
- 1—4¾" square for position A
- 8—2" squares for position B
- 1—4¼" square, cutting it diagonally twice in an X for a total of 4 triangles for position D
- 4—2⅜" squares, cutting each in half diagonally for a total of 8 triangles for position C

From assorted dark prints, cut:
- 8—2⅜" squares, cutting each in half diagonally for a total of 16 triangles for position C

From assorted medium prints, cut:
- 4—2⅜" squares, cutting each in half diagonally for a total of 8 triangles for position C

1. Referring to Diagram 1 for placement, sew together one gold print B square and two medium print C triangles to make a corner unit. Press the seam allowances toward the gold print C triangles. Repeat to make a total of four corner units.

5. Lay out the center unit, the eight triangle-squares, the four Flying Geese units, and the remaining four gold print B squares in sections as shown in Diagram 5. Sew together the pieces in each section. Press the seam allowances in one direction. Sew the top and bottom sections to the top and bottom edges of the center unit. Then join the side sections to the side edges of the center unit to make a Sunshine block. Press all seam allowances toward the outside edges. The pieced Sunshine block should measure 9½" square, including the seam allowances.

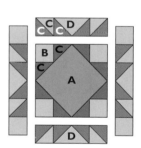

Diagram 5

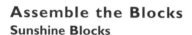

Friendship Star Blocks

Each Friendship Star block needs only two prints, one for the background and one for the star (see Diagram 8). In some cases the lighter print is used as the background fabric, while in other cases it serves as the star fabric.

The cutting and assembly instructions that follow are for making one Friendship Star block. Repeat to make a total of 25 Friendship Star blocks.

From background print, cut:
- 4—2" squares
- 2—2×3½" rectangles

From star print, cut:
- 2—2" squares
- 1—2×5" rectangle

1. Use a quilter's pencil to mark a diagonal line on the wrong side of two background print 2" squares and the two star print 2" squares. (To prevent the fabric from stretching as you draw the lines, place 220-grit sandpaper under the squares.)

2. Align a marked star print 2" square with one end of a background print 2×3½" rectangle (see Diagram 6, noting the direction of the drawn diagonal line). Stitch on the drawn line. Trim the seam allowance to ¼" and press the attached triangle open to make a rectangle unit A. The pieced rectangle unit should still measure 2×3½", including the seam allowances. Repeat to make a second rectangle unit A.

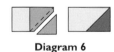

Diagram 6

Diagram 7

3. Align a marked background print 2" square with each end of the star print 2×5" rectangle (see Diagram 7, noting the direction of the drawn diagonal lines). Stitch on the drawn lines. Trim the seam allowances to ¼" and press the attached triangles open to make a rectangle unit B. The pieced rectangle unit should still measure 2×5", including the seam allowances.

4. Referring to Diagram 8 for placement, lay out the rectangle units and the two remaining background print 2" squares in three rows.

Diagram 8

Sew together the pieces in the top and bottom rows. Then join the rows to make a Friendship Star block. Press the seam allowances in one direction. The pieced Friendship Star block should measure 5" square, including the seam allowances.

Bear's Paw Blocks

Each Bear's Paw block requires only two prints, one for the background and one for the bear's paw (see Diagram 9). In some blocks the lighter print is used for the background fabric, while in other cases it is used for the bear's paw.

The cutting and assembly instructions that follow are for making one Bear's Paw block. Repeat to make a total of 25 Bear's Paw blocks.

From background print, cut:
- 2—2⅜" squares, cutting each in half diagonally for a total of 4 triangles
- 1—2" square

From bear's paw print, cut:
- 1—3½" square
- 2—2⅜" squares, cutting each in half diagonally for a total of 4 triangles

1. Sew together one background print triangle and one bear's paw print triangle to make a triangle-square. Press the seam allowance toward the darker print. The pieced triangle-square should measure 2" square, including the seam allowances. Repeat to make a total of four triangle-squares.

2. Referring to Diagram 9, lay out four triangle-squares, a background print 2" square, and a bear's paw print 3½" square. Sew together the squares in sections. Then join the sections to make a Bear's Paw block. The pieced Bear's Paw block should measure 5" square, including the seam allowances.

Diagram 9

Log Cabin Blocks

The cutting and assembly instructions on *page 40* are for making one Log Cabin block. Repeat to make a second Log Cabin block.

continued

From assorted print scraps, cut:
- 1—2½×3" rectangle for position 1
- 1—1½×3" rectangle for position 2
- 1—1½×3½" rectangle for position 3
- 1—1½×4" rectangle for position 4
- 1—1½×4½" rectangle for position 5
- 2—1×5" rectangles for positions 6 and 7

Referring to Diagram 10 for placement, align long edges and sew together print rectangles for positions 1 and 2. Press the seam allowance toward the position 2 rectangle. Add print rectangles for positions 3 through 7 in numerical order to make a Log Cabin block. The pieced Log Cabin block should measure 5½×5", including the seam allowances.

Diagram 10

Ohio Star Blocks

To make the Ohio Stars "float" in the outer border (see the photograph on *page 38*), the same two tan prints used for the outer border were used for the Ohio Star blocks' backgrounds. Besides a tan print for the background, each Ohio Star block also takes two other prints—one for the star center and one for the star points.

The cutting and assembly instructions that follow are for making one Ohio Star block. Repeat to make a total of 20 Ohio Star blocks, 10 using tan print No. 1 as the background and 10 using tan print No. 2 as the background.

From tan print Nos. 1 or 2, cut:
- 4—2" squares
- 4—2×3½" rectangles

From star center print, cut:
- 1—3½" square

From star points print, cut:
- 8—2" squares

1. For accurate sewing lines, use a quilter's pencil to mark a diagonal line on the wrong side of the eight star points print 2" squares.

2. Align a marked star points print 2" square with one end of a tan print 2×3½" rectangle (see Diagram 11; note the placement of the marked diagonal line). Stitch on the marked line; trim

away the excess fabric, leaving a ¼" seam allowance. Press the attached triangle open.

Diagram 11

3. In the same manner, align a second marked star points print 2" square with the opposite end of the rectangle (see Diagram 11, again noting the placement of the marked diagonal line). Stitch on the marked line; trim and press as before to make a Flying Geese unit. The pieced Flying Geese unit should still measure 2×3½", including the seam allowances.

4. Repeat steps 2 and 3 to make a total of four Flying Geese units.

5. Referring to Diagram 12, lay out the Flying Geese units, a star center print 3½" square, and four tan print 2" squares in three horizontal rows. Sew together the pieces in each row. Press the seam allowances toward the squares. Then join the rows to make an Ohio Star block. Press the seam allowances in one direction. The pieced Ohio Star block should measure 6½" square, including the seam allowances.

Diagram 12

Assemble the Quilt Center

Referring to Diagram 13 *opposite*, join four Sunshine blocks in pairs. Press the seam allowances in opposite directions. Then join the pairs to make the quilt center. The pieced quilt center should measure 18½" square, including the seam allowances.

Add the Borders

Diagram 13 *opposite* includes borders 1 through 4; refer to it for block placement.

Border 1

From assorted print scraps, cut:
- 20—1½"-wide strips in lengths between 6" and 8"

1. Cut and piece the assorted print strips, using diagonal seams, to make the following:
   - 2—1½×20½" border strips
   - 2—1½×18½" border strips

2. Sew the short pieced border strips to opposite edges of the pieced quilt center. Then add the long pieced border strips to the remaining edges of the pieced quilt center. Press all seam allowances toward the pieced border. The pieced quilt center should now measure 20½" square, including the seam allowances.

Border 2
From assorted print scraps, cut:
- 12—2×2½" rectangles

1. Aligning long edges, sew together three rectangles to make a rectangle unit. The rectangle unit should measure 2½×5", including the seam allowances. Repeat to make a total of four rectangle units.

2. For the right-hand border unit, sew together four Friendship Star blocks and one rectangle unit. The pieced right-hand border unit should measure 5×20½", including the seam allowances. Add the pieced border unit to the right-hand edge of the pieced quilt center.

3. For the left-hand border unit, sew together four Bear's Paw blocks and one rectangle unit. The pieced left-hand border unit should measure 5×20½", including the seam allowances. Add the pieced border unit to the left-hand edge of the pieced quilt center.

4. For the top border unit, sew together six Friendship Star blocks and one rectangle unit. The pieced top border unit should measure 5×29½", including the seam allowances. Add the pieced top border unit to the top edge of the pieced quilt center.

5. For the bottom border unit, sew together six Bear's Paw blocks and one rectangle unit. The pieced bottom border unit should measure 5×29½", including the seam allowances. Add the pieced bottom border unit to the bottom edge of the pieced quilt center. The pieced quilt center should now measure 29½" square, including the seam allowances.

Border 3
From black star print, cut:
- 2—2×32½" border strips
- 2—2×29½" border strips

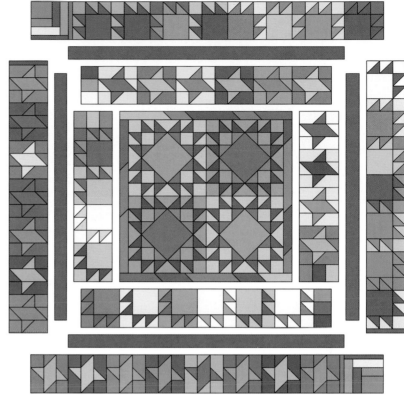

Diagram 13

Sew the short border strips to opposite edges of the pieced quilt center. Then add the long border strips to the remaining edges of the pieced quilt center. Press all seam allowances toward the black star print border. The pieced quilt center should now measure 32½" square, including the seam allowances.

Border 4
From assorted print scraps, cut:
- 2—1×5" rectangles

1. For the right-hand border unit, sew together seven Bear's Paw blocks and one assorted print 1×5" rectangle. The pieced right-hand border unit should measure 5×32½", including the seam allowances. Add the pieced border unit to the right-hand edge of the pieced quilt center.

2. For the left-hand border unit, sew together seven Friendship Star blocks and one assorted print 1×5" rectangle. The pieced left-hand border unit should measure 5×32½", including the seam allowances. Add the pieced border unit to the left-hand edge of the pieced quilt center.

continued

3. For the top border unit, sew together eight Bear's Paw blocks and one Log Cabin block. The pieced top border unit should measure 5×41½", including the seam allowances. Add the pieced top border unit to the top edge of the pieced quilt center.

4. For the bottom border unit, sew together eight Friendship Star blocks and one Log Cabin block. The pieced bottom border unit should measure 5×41½", including the seam allowances. Add the pieced bottom border unit to the bottom edge of the quilt center. The quilt center should measure 41½" square, including the seam allowances.

Border 5

Referring to the photograph on *page 38*, note that one half of this border uses tan print No. 1; the other half uses tan print No. 2.

From *each* tan print, cut:
• 4—4½×8" rectangles
• 2—3½×9½" rectangles
• 2—3½×6½" rectangles
• 8—2×6½" rectangles

From black star print, cut:
• 8—2×16½" rectangles

1. Referring to Diagram 14, Unit B, lay out two 2×6½" rectangles and one 4½×8" rectangle in tan print No. 1, two Ohio Star blocks that were pieced with tan print No. 1, and a black star print 2×16½" rectangle; join.

2. Referring to Diagram 14, Unit D, lay out two 2×6½" rectangles and one 4½×8" rectangle in tan print No. 2, two Ohio Star blocks that were pieced with tan print No. 2, and a black star print 2×16½" rectangle; sew together.

3. Join pieced units B and D to opposite edges of a Sunshine block (Unit C) to make the top border unit. The pieced top border unit should measure 9½×41½", including the seam allowances.

4. Repeat steps 1 through 3 to make the bottom border unit. Add the pieced border units to the top and bottom edges of the quilt center.

5. Referring to Diagram 14, units A and B, and the photograph on *page 38* for placement, lay out and sew together two 2×6½" rectangles, one 3½×6½" rectangle, one 3½×9½" rectangle, and one 4½×8" rectangle in tan print No. 2; three Ohio Star blocks that were pieced with tan print No. 2; and a black star print 2×16½" rectangle.

6. Referring to Diagram 14, units D and E, lay out and sew together two 2×6½" rectangles, one 3½×6½" rectangle, one 3½×9½" rectangle, and one 4½×8" rectangle in tan print No. 1; three Ohio Star blocks that were pieced with tan print No. 1; and a black star print 2×16½" rectangle.

7. Join the pieced units A/B and D/E to opposite sides of a Sunshine block (Unit C) to make a side border unit. The pieced side border unit should measure 9½×59½", including the seam allowances.

8. Repeat steps 5 through 7 to make a second side border unit. Add the pieced side border units to the side edges of the pieced quilt center to complete the quilt top. The pieced quilt top should now measure 59½" square, including the seam allowances.

Complete the Quilt

From black star print, cut:
• 6—2½×42" binding strips

1. Layer the quilt top, batting, and backing according to the instructions in Quilter's Schoolhouse, which begins on *page 150*. Quilt as desired.

2. Use the black star print 2½×42" strips to bind the quilt according to the instructions in Quilter's Schoolhouse.

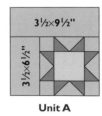

Unit A

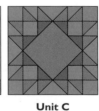 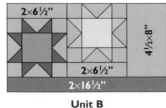

Unit B

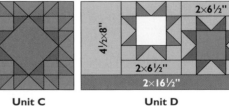

Unit C

Unit D

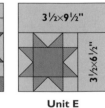

Unit E

Diagram 14

BED QUILT AND PILLOWCASES

This blue-and-cream quilt showcases the Friendship Star block from the "Twilight" pattern. Tea-dye the shirting prints before cutting them for an old-fashioned look.

Materials for Twin Quilt

16—3/8-yard pieces of assorted blue-and-cream prints for blocks, setting squares, and border

4—7/8-yard pieces of assorted cream shirting prints for blocks

1½ yards of dark blue print for border and binding

5½ yards of backing fabric

71×98" of quilt batting

Finished quilt top: 64½×91½"

continued

Assemble the Blocks

Referring to Assemble the Blocks—Friendship Star Blocks on *page 39*, use two blue-and-cream print 2" squares, one blue-and-cream print 2×5" rectangle, four cream shirting print 2" squares, and two cream shirting print 2×3½" rectangles to make a Friendship Star block. Repeat to make a total of 124 Friendship Star blocks.

Assemble the Quilt Center

1. Referring to the photograph *left* for placement, lay out the 124 pieced Friendship Star blocks and 123 assorted blue-and-cream print 5" setting squares in 19 horizontal rows.

2. Sew together the blocks in each row. Press the seam allowances toward the setting squares.

3. Join the rows to complete the quilt center. Press the seam allowances in one direction. The pieced quilt center should measure 59×86", including the seam allowances.

Add the Border

1. Cut and piece the dark blue print 3½×42" strips to make the following:
   - 2—3½×92" border strips
   - 2—3½×59" border strips

2. Sew the short border strips to the top and bottom edges of the quilt center. Add the long border strips to each side edge of the quilt center to complete the quilt top. Press the seam allowances toward the border.

Complete the Quilt

1. Layer the quilt top, batting, and backing according to the instructions in Quilter's Schoolhouse, which begins on *page 150*. Quilt as desired.

2. Use the dark blue print 2½×42" strips to bind the quilt according to the instructions in Quilter's Schoolhouse.

Cut the Fabrics

To make the best use of your fabrics, cut the pieces in the order that follows.

From *each* assorted blue-and-cream print, cut:
- 8—5" squares (you'll have 5 leftover squares)
- 8—2×5" rectangles (you'll have 4 leftover rectangles)
- 16—2" squares (you'll have 8 leftover squares)

From *each* assorted cream shirting print, cut:
- 62—2×3½" rectangles
- 124—2" squares

From dark blue print, cut:
- 8—3½×42" strips for border
- 8—2½×42" binding strips

Materials for Two Pillowcases

6—1/8-yard pieces of assorted blue-and-cream prints

2⅜ yards of cream shirting print

¼ yard of dark blue print for sashing

Finished pillowcase: fits a standard 20×26" or 20×28" pillow

Cut the Fabrics

To make the best use of your fabrics, cut the pieces in the order that follows:

From *each* assorted blue-and-cream print, cut:
- 3—2×5" rectangles (you'll have 2 leftover rectangles)
- 6—2" squares (you'll have 4 leftover squares)

From cream shirting print, cut:
- 2—22×42½" rectangles
- 2—12½×42½" strips
- 32—2×3½" rectangles
- 64—2" squares

From dark blue print, cut:
- 4—1¼×42½" sashing strips
- 16—1¼×5" sashing strips

Assemble the Blocks

Referring to Assemble the Blocks—Friendship Star Blocks on *page 39*, use two blue-and-cream print 2" squares, one blue-and-cream print 2×5" rectangle, four cream shirting print 2" squares, and two cream shirting print 2×3½" rectangles to make a Friendship Star block. Repeat to make a total of 16 Friendship Star blocks.

Assemble the Border

1. Join eight pieced Friendship Star blocks and eight dark blue print 1¼×5" sashing strips to make a border strip. Press the seam allowances toward the sashing strips. Repeat to make a second border strip.

2. Sew the dark blue print 1¼×42½" sashing strips to the long edges of each pieced border strip. Press the seam allowances toward the long sashing strips.

Assemble the Pillowcases

1. Referring to the Pillowcase Assembly Diagram for placement, lay out the pieces for one pillowcase. Sew together the pieces, pressing the seams away from the pieced border strip.

2. Fold the pieced unit in half along the center fold line and sew together the long edges and the short edges farthest from the pieced border strip to make a pillowcase. Press the seam allowances to one side. Turn the pillowcase right side out.

3. Fold the unfinished edge under ¼" and press. Fold the same edge under 9", covering the pieced border and extending the edge a scant ¼" beyond it. From the right side, topstitch the folded section along the dark blue sashing strips.

4. Repeat steps 1 through 3 to make a second pillowcase.

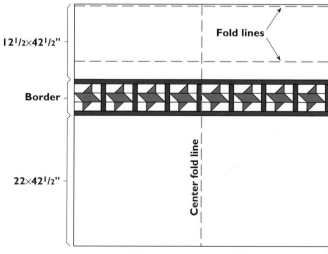

Pillowcase Assembly Diagram

FLORAL THROW

This quilt pattern features a center panel that lets you use a favorite print you can't bring yourself to cut up.

Materials

1⅓ yards of cream print for blocks

⅝ yard total of assorted dark red prints for blocks

2⅓ yards of light green print for borders and binding

1⅔ yards of floral print for center panel

3⅝ yards of backing fabric

65×83" of quilt batting

Finished quilt top: 59×77"

Cut the Fabrics

To make the best use of your fabrics, cut the pieces in the order that follows. The light green border and binding strips are cut the length of the fabric (parallel to the selvage).

From cream print, cut:
- 52—3½" squares
- 104—2⅜" squares, cutting each in half diagonally for a total of 208 triangles
- 52—2" squares

From assorted dark red prints, cut:
- 104—2⅜" squares, cutting each in half diagonally for a total of 208 triangles

From light green print, cut:
- 2—3×77½" outer border strips
- 2—3×63½" inner border strips
- 2—3×54½" outer border strips
- 7—2½×42" strips for binding
- 2—3×40½" inner border strips

From floral print, cut:
- 1—40½×58½" center rectangle

Assemble the Blocks

Referring to Assemble the Blocks—Bear's Paw Blocks on *page 39*, use four cream print triangles, one cream print 2" square, one cream print 3½" square, and four dark red print triangles to make a Bear's Paw block. Repeat to make a total of 52 Bear's Paw blocks.

Add the Borders

1. Sew the light green print 3×40½" inner border strips to the short edges of the floral print center rectangle. Add the light green print 3×63½" inner border strips to the long edges of the quilt center. Press the seam allowances toward the inner border.

2. Referring to the photograph *above right* for placement, lay out 10 pieced Bear's Paw blocks; sew together to make a short pieced middle border strip. Repeat to make a second short pieced middle border strip. Press the seam allowances in one direction. Sew the short pieced middle border strips to the short edges of the quilt center. Press the seam allowances toward the inner border.

3. Sew together 16 blocks to make a long pieced middle border strip. Repeat to make a second

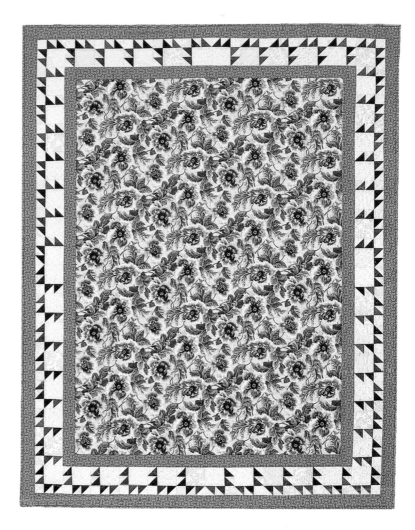

long pieced middle border strip. Press the seam allowances in one direction. Sew the long pieced middle border strips to the long edges of the quilt center. Press the seam allowances toward the inner border.

4. Sew the light green print 3×54½" outer border strips to the short edges of the quilt center. Then join the light green print 3×77½" outer border strips to the long edges of the quilt center to complete the quilt top. Press all seam allowances toward the outer border.

Complete the Quilt

1. Layer the quilt top, batting, and backing according to the instructions in Quilter's Schoolhouse, which begins on *page 150*. Quilt as desired.

2. Use the light green print 2½×42" strips to bind the quilt according to the instructions in Quilter's Schoolhouse.

Sisters' *Starberries*

Sisters Claudia Fix and Dana Barnett combined

Claudia's appliqué skills and Dana's favorite fabrics to create

this summer-sweet wall hanging.

Materials

6—$\frac{1}{3}$-yard pieces of assorted dark red prints for blocks and appliqués

6—$\frac{1}{8}$-yard pieces of assorted pink prints for blocks and appliqués

6—$\frac{1}{3}$-yard pieces of assorted white prints for blocks

$\frac{5}{8}$ yard of pink plaid for appliqué foundation

$1\frac{5}{8}$ yards of yellow stripe for appliqué foundation, appliqués, and pieced border

$\frac{5}{8}$ yard of purple check for appliqué foundation

$1\frac{5}{8}$ yards of solid green for appliqués, inner border, and binding

Scraps of assorted green, lilac, and pink prints for appliqués

$\frac{1}{4}$ yard of dark pink print for middle border

1 yard of lilac print for pieced border

$4\frac{1}{4}$ yards of backing fabric

74×78" of quilt batting

Finished quilt top: 68×72"
Finished block: 8" square

Quantities specified for 44/45"-wide, 100% cotton fabrics. All measurements include a $\frac{1}{4}$" seam allowance. Sew with right sides together unless otherwise stated.

continued

Cut the Fabrics

To make the best use of your fabrics, cut the pieces in the order that follows. Cut the solid green inner border strips the length of the fabric (parallel to the selvage).

The patterns are on *Pattern Sheet 1*. To make templates of the patterns, follow the instructions in Quilter's Schoolhouse, which begins on *page 150*.

From *each* assorted dark red print, cut:
- 4—2⅞" squares, cutting each in half diagonally for a total of 8 triangles
- 32—2½" squares

From *each* assorted pink print, cut:
- 4—2⅞" squares, cutting each in half diagonally for a total of 8 triangles
- 8—2½" squares

From remaining dark red and pink print scraps, cut:
- 12 of Pattern B

From *each* assorted white print, cut:
- 16—2½×4½" rectangles
- 16—2½" squares

From pink plaid, cut:
- 2—6½×42" strips

From yellow stripe, cut:
- 2—8½×42" strips
- 7—4½×42" strips for pieced border
- 6 of Pattern C

From purple check, cut:
- 2—6½×42" strips

From solid green, cut:
- 2—2×52½" inner border strips
- 2—2×51½" inner border strips
- 7—2½×42" binding strips
- 1—9×22" rectangle, cutting it into enough 1"-wide bias strips to total 104" in length for vine appliqués (For specific instructions on cutting bias strips, see Quilter's Schoolhouse.)
- 6 of Pattern D
- 12 of Pattern E

From assorted green print scraps, cut:
- 16 of Pattern A

From assorted lilac print scraps, cut:
- 6 *each* of patterns C and F

From assorted pink print scraps, cut:
- 6 of Pattern G

From dark pink print, cut:
- 6—1×42" strips for middle border

From lilac print, cut:
- 7—4½×42" strips for pieced border

Assemble the Star Blocks

The following instructions are for piecing one star block. Repeat these steps to make a total of 24 star blocks. The quiltmakers used just one dark red print, one pink print, and one white print in each star block.

1. Sew together one dark red print triangle and one pink print triangle to make a triangle-square (see Diagram 1). Press the seam allowance toward the dark red print triangle. The pieced triangle-square should measure 2½" square, including the seam allowances. Repeat to make a second triangle-square.

Diagram 1   **Diagram 2**

2. Referring to Diagram 2 for placement, sew together the two triangle-squares and two pink print 2½" squares in pairs. Press the seam allowances toward the pink print squares. Sew together the pairs to make the block center. Press the seam allowance in one direction. The pieced block center should measure 4½" square, including the seam allowances.

3. For accurate sewing lines, use a quilter's pencil to mark a diagonal line on the wrong side of eight dark red print 2½" squares. (To prevent your fabric from stretching as you draw the lines, place 220-grit sandpaper under the squares.)

4. With right sides together, align a marked dark red print 2½" square with one end of a white print 2½×4½" rectangle (see Diagram 3; note the placement of the marked diagonal line). Stitch on the marked line; trim away the excess fabric, leaving a ¼" seam allowance. Press the attached triangle open.

Diagram 3

5. In the same manner, align a second marked dark red print 2½" square with the opposite end of the white print rectangle (see Diagram 3, again noting the placement of the marked diagonal line). Stitch on the marked line; trim and press as before to make a Flying Geese unit. The pieced Flying Geese unit should still measure 2½×4½", including the seam allowances.

6. Repeat steps 4 and 5 to make a total of four Flying Geese units.

7. Referring to Diagram 4, sew a Flying Geese unit to opposite edges of the pieced block center. Press the seam allowances toward the block center.

Diagram 4

8. Sew a white print 2½" square to each end of the remaining Flying Geese units. Press the seam allowances toward the white print squares. Then join the units to the remaining edges of the pieced block center to make a star block. Press the seam allowances in one direction. The pieced star block should measure 8½" square, including the seam allowances.

Appliqué the Foundations

1. Cut and piece the pink plaid 6½×42" strips to make the following:
   • 1—6½×48½" appliqué foundation

2. Referring to the photograph on *page 48* for placement, arrange the following appliqué pieces atop the pink plaid appliqué foundation: one solid green 52"-long bias strip, eight green print A leaves, six pink and dark red print B flowers, and the six lilac print C flower centers; baste in place.

Sisters' Starberries Quilt
optional sizes

If you'd like to make this quilt in a size other than for a wall hanging, use the information *below*.

Alternate quilt sizes	Crib/Lap	Queen/King
Number of star blocks	9	54
Number of blocks wide	3	9
Number of rows	5	11
Number and finished size of appliqué rows	two 6×24"	two 6×72", three 8×72"
Finished size	44×56"	92×104"
Yardage requirements		
Assorted dark red prints	¾ yard total	2¾ yards total
Assorted pink prints	½ yard total	1⅓ yards total
Assorted white prints	¾ yard total	3 yards total
Pink plaid	⅜ yard	⅝ yard
Yellow stripe	1 yard	3 yards
Purple check	⅜ yard	⅝ yard
Solid green	1¼ yards	2½ yards
Assorted green, lilac, and pink prints	scraps	scraps
Dark pink print	¼ yard	⅓ yard
Lilac print	⅞ yard	1½ yards
Backing	2⅞ yards	8¼ yards
Batting	50×62"	98×110"

continued

3. Using matching threads and a slip stitch, appliqué the pieces in place. Always work from the bottom appliqué piece to the top.

4. Cut and piece the yellow stripe 8½×42" strips to make the following:
   • 1—8½×48½" appliqué foundation

5. Referring to the photograph on *page 48*, arrange the following appliqué pieces atop the yellow stripe appliqué foundation: the six solid green D stems, the 12 solid green E leaves, the six lilac print F flowers, and the six pink print G flower centers; baste in place. Appliqué the pieces in place as before.

6. Cut and piece the purple check 6½×42" strips to make the following:
   • 1—6½×48½" appliqué foundation

7. Referring to the photograph on *page 48*, arrange the following pieces atop the purple check appliqué foundation: the remaining solid green 52"-long bias strip, eight green print A leaves, six pink and dark red print B flowers, and the six yellow stripe C flower centers; baste in place. Appliqué the pieces in place as before.

Assemble the Quilt Center

1. Referring to the photograph on *page 48*, lay out the 24 star blocks in four rows. Sew together the blocks in each row. Press the seam allowances in one direction.

2. Sew together the four block rows and the three appliquéd foundations to make the quilt center. Press the seam allowances in one direction. The pieced quilt center should measure 48½×52½", including the seam allowances.

Assemble and Add the Borders

1. Sew the solid green 2×52½" inner border strips to the side edges of the pieced quilt center. Then join the solid green 2×51½" inner border strips to the top and bottom edges of the pieced quilt center. Press all seam allowances toward the solid green border.

optional colors

"There aren't always large square areas in a house," says quilt tester Laura Boehnke, so she turned the horizontal appliqué rows into vertical ones and centered them between star blocks to make this wall hanging. Perfect for a two-story entry hall, this design is also great for a lap-size quilt. Simply alternate flower and vine strips to a desired width, then add enough star blocks to go across the top and bottom, suggests Laura.

Although she used several earth-tone prints for this color option, Laura says, "I could see using really funky, bright prints with these flowers."

2. Cut and piece the dark pink print 1×42" strips to make the following:
- 2—1×55½" middle border strips
- 2—1×52½" middle border strips

3. Sew the long middle border strips to the side edges of the pieced quilt center. Then add the short middle border strips to the top and bottom edges of the pieced quilt center. Press all seam allowances toward the dark pink print border.

4. Sew together a yellow stripe 4½×42" strip and a lilac print 4½×42" strip to make a strip set (see Diagram 5). Press the seam allowance toward the lilac print strip. Repeat to make a total of seven strip sets. Cut the strips sets into sixty-two 4½"-wide segments.

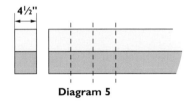

Diagram 5

5. Referring to the photograph on *page 48*, sew together 13 Step 4 segments, alternating the color positions, to make the top outer border unit. Press the seam allowances in one direction. Repeat to make the bottom outer border unit. Sew the outer border units to the top and bottom edges of the pieced quilt center. Press the seam allowances toward the pieced border.

6. Join 18 Step 4 segments, alternating the color positions, to make a side outer border unit. Repeat to make a second side outer border unit. Sew the side outer border units to the side edges of the pieced quilt center to complete the quilt top. Press the seam allowances toward the pieced border.

Complete the Quilt

1. Layer the quilt top, batting, and backing according to the instructions in Quilter's Schoolhouse, which begins on *page 150*. Quilt as desired.

2. Use the solid green 2½×42" strips to bind the quilt according to the instructions in Quilter's Schoolhouse.

APPLIQUÉD VALANCE

Give a valance personality with a row

of yellow and white appliqués.

Materials

Scraps of yellow and white prints for appliqués

Purchased 81×14" valance

Lightweight fusible web

Finished valance: 81×14"

continued

1. Lay the fusible web, paper side up, over the patterns. With a pencil, trace each pattern the number of times specified in Step 2, leaving ½" between tracings. Cut out the pieces roughly ¼" outside the traced lines.

2. Following the manufacturer's instructions, press the fusible-web shapes onto the back of the designated fabrics; let cool. Cut out the pieces on the drawn lines. Peel off the paper backings.

From yellow print scraps, cut:
• 19 of Pattern B
From white print scraps, cut:
• 19 of Pattern C

Cut and Stitch the Appliqués

To make the best use of your fabrics, cut the pieces in the order that follows. *Note:* To make this project for an alternate window size, adjust the number of appliqués as desired.

To use fusible web for appliquéing, as was done in this project, use the following steps. This project uses "Sisters' Starberries" patterns, which are on *Pattern Sheet 1.*

3. Position the prepared appliqué pieces on the valance; fuse in place.

4. Using color-coordinated embroidery threads, machine-satin-stitch around each appliqué piece.

Sisters' Starberries

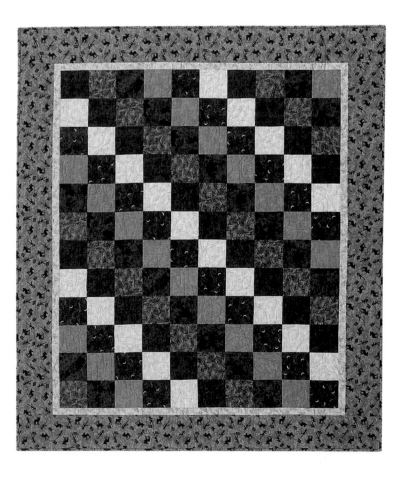

FLANNEL THROW

Nature-inspired prints accent this lodge-look quilt that you can stitch up in a weekend.

Materials

6—½-yard pieces of assorted blue, green, and beige print flannels

1⅝ yards of tan print flannel for inner border

1⅞ yards of green print flannel for outer border and binding

3¼ yards of backing fabric

58×66" of quilt batting

Finished quilt top: 52×60"

Cut the Fabrics

To make the best use of your fabrics, cut the pieces in the order that follows.

The border and binding strips are cut the length of the fabric (parallel to the selvage).

From *each* assorted blue, green, and beige print, cut:
• 20—4½" squares

From tan print, cut:
• 2—1½×50½" inner border strips
• 2—1½×40½" inner border strips

From green print, cut:
• 4—2½×63" binding strips
• 2—5½×60½" outer border strips
• 2—5½×42½" outer border strips

Assemble the Quilt Center

1. Referring to the photograph *opposite* for placement, lay out the 120 squares in 12 horizontal rows. Sew together the squares in each row. Press the seam allowances in one direction, alternating the direction with each row.

2. Join the rows to complete the quilt center. Press the seam allowances in one direction. The pieced quilt center should measure 40½×48½", including the seam allowances.

Add the Borders

1. Sew the tan print 1½×40½" inner border strips to the top and bottom edges of the quilt center. Add the tan print 1½×50½" inner border strips to the side edges of the quilt center. Press the seam allowances toward the inner border.

2. Sew the green print 5½×42½" outer border strips to the top and bottom edges of the quilt center. Then join the green print 5½×60½" outer border strips to the side edges of the quilt center to complete the quilt top. Press all seam allowances toward the outer border.

Complete the Quilt

1. Layer the quilt top, batting, and backing according to the instructions in Quilter's Schoolhouse, which begins on *page 150*. Quilt as desired.

2. Use the green print 2½×63" strips to bind the quilt according to the instructions in Quilter's Schoolhouse.

TEXAS *Stars*

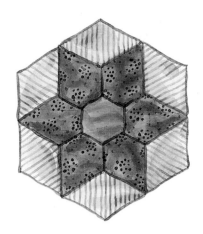

The homespun fabric that designer Marti Michell used for the appliqué foundations complements both the quilt's folk art style and the 1920s and '30s reproduction prints she chose for the stars. Marti suggests re-creating the project in reproduction fabrics or funky, bright prints. For a banner version using bright colors, see page 62.

Materials

- 21—4" squares of assorted yellow, gold, and rust prints for blocks
- 21—10×13" pieces of assorted green, blue, brown, red, and gold prints for blocks
- 11—11×18" pieces of assorted ivory prints for blocks
- 1⅝ yards of burgundy print for setting units and vine appliqués
- ⅝ yard of ecru print for setting units
- 5 yards of red-and-green plaid for appliqué foundations
- ⅔ yard of green print for vine appliqués
- 1⅝ yards of dark green print for vine appliqués and binding
- ⅝ yard of gold check for vine appliqués
- 30—8×10" pieces of assorted brown, rust, red, green, and gold prints for leaf appliqués
- 7½ yards of backing fabric
- 90×116" of quilt batting

Finished quilt top: 83½×110"
Finished Texas Star block: 10½×12"

Quantities specified for 44/45"-wide, 100% cotton fabrics. All measurements include a ¼" seam allowance. Sew with right sides together unless otherwise stated.

continued

Designer Notes

Designer Marti Michell employs several timesaving techniques when cutting pattern pieces for projects such as this one. For example, if several fabrics are to be cut the same way, she stacks the fabrics with the right sides facing one direction, then cuts as directed. When cutting with templates, Marti first cuts her fabrics into strips, stacks the strips right sides up, places the template on the stacked strips, and cuts around the template with her rotary cutter multiple times (see diagrams 1 and 2).

The following instructions reflect Marti's techniques.

Diagram 1   **Diagram 2**

Cut the Fabrics

To make the best use of your fabrics, cut the pieces in the order that follows. The red-and-green plaid appliqué foundation rectangles are cut the length of the fabric (parallel to the selvage).

The patterns are on *Pattern Sheet 2*. To make templates of the patterns, follow the instructions in Quilter's Schoolhouse, which begins on *page 150*.

From *each* assorted yellow, gold, and rust print, cut:
- 1 of Pattern A

From *each* assorted green, blue, brown, red, and gold print, cut:
- 2—4⅜×13" strips, cutting 3 of Pattern B from each strip for a total of 126

From *each* assorted ivory print, cut:
- 3—3⅛×18" strips, cutting 4 of Pattern C from each strip for a total of 132 (you'll have 6 leftover C pieces)

From burgundy print, cut:
- 19—3⅛×27" strips, cutting 7 of Pattern D from each strip for a total of 133 (you'll have 1 leftover D piece)
- 1—20" square, cutting it into ⅞"-wide bias strips; join the bias strips into a 420"-long vine strip (For specific instructions on cutting bias strips, see Quilter's Schoolhouse.)

From ecru print, cut:
- 12—3⅛×18" strips, cutting 4 of Pattern D from each strip for a total of 48

From red-and-green plaid, cut:
- 4—13½×84½" rectangles for appliqué foundations
- 2—13½×84" rectangles for appliqué foundations

From green print, cut:
- 1—20" square, cutting it into ⅞"-wide bias strips; join the bias strips into a 420"-long vine strip
- 1—16" square, cutting it into 1"-wide bias strips; join the bias strips into two 120"-long vine strips

From dark green print, cut:
- 10—2½×42" binding strips
- 1—30" square, cutting it into 1"-wide bias strips; join the bias strips into two 330"-long vine strips

From gold check, cut:
- 1—20" square, cutting it into ⅞"-wide bias strips; join the bias strips into a 420"-long vine strip

From assorted brown, rust, red, green, and gold prints, cut:
- 6 *each* of patterns E, F, G, H, I, and L
- 8 *each* of patterns J and K
- 24 of Pattern M

Assemble the Texas Star Blocks

1. To make one Texas Star block you'll need one yellow, gold, or rust print A hexagon, six matching B pieces, and six matching C diamonds.

2. Referring to Diagram 3 for placement, join the A hexagon and one B piece; press the seam allowance toward the hexagon. Set in a second B piece. (For specific instructions on setting in seams, see Quilter's Schoolhouse, which begins on *page 150*.) Press the seam allowance toward the B piece. Add the remaining B pieces to the hexagon in the same manner, pressing the seam allowances in alternate directions.

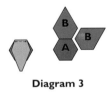

Diagram 3

3. Referring to Diagram 4, set a C diamond into a pair of B pieces. Marti recommends sewing from the center dot (marked on the pattern) to one outer edge, then starting again at the center dot and sewing to the other outer edge. Press the seams in one direction and all other seams in the opposite direction. Pressing after sewing each seam makes adding the next piece easier. If you're hand-piecing, it is not necessary to stop

and cut the thread between seams; you can stop, finger-press, reposition pieces, then continue sewing.

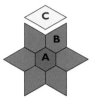

Diagram 4

Diagram 5

4. Add the remaining C pieces in the same manner to make a Texas Star block (see Diagram 5); thoroughly press the completed block.

5. Repeat steps 1 through 4 to make a total of 21 Texas Star blocks.

Assemble the Setting Units

1. Referring to Diagram 6, lay out three burgundy print D triangles and one ecru print D triangle. First sew together two burgundy print triangles and the ecru print triangle; press the seam allowances toward the burgundy print triangles. Then add the third burgundy print triangle to complete a triangle setting unit. Press the seam allowance toward the burgundy print triangle. Repeat to make a total of 36 triangle setting units.

Diagram 6

Diagram 7

2. Referring to Diagram 7, sew together two burgundy print D triangles and an ecru print D triangle to make a partial setting unit. Press the seam allowances toward the burgundy print triangles. Repeat to make a total of 12 partial setting units.

Assemble the Texas Star Rows

1. Arrange the Texas Star blocks into three vertical rows of seven blocks each (see the photograph *above right* for color placement ideas).

2. Once you're pleased with the block arrangement, sew a triangle setting unit to opposite edges of the center block in each row (see Diagram 8).

Press the seam allowances toward the triangle setting units. Repeat with all but the top and bottom blocks in each row.

Texas Stars

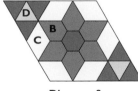

Diagram 8

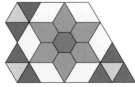

Diagram 9

3. Referring to Diagram 9 for placement, sew two partial setting units and one triangle setting unit to the top block in each row. Repeat with the bottom block in each row.

continued

4. Referring to Diagram 10, sew together the seven units in each row. Press the seam allowances in one direction. (The edges of the partial setting units will be trimmed once the quilt center is assembled.) Each pieced block row should measure 11×84½", including the seam allowances.

Diagram 10

Appliqué the Center Panels

Marti chose to appliqué the two center panels before assembling the quilt top. She left excess vine at the ends of the center panels to appliqué to the outer panels later. Marti suggests working on a long table to accommodate the length of the panels.

1. Intertwine a green print 1×120" vine strip and a dark green print 1×330" vine strip down the inner third of a red-and-green plaid 13½×84½" rectangle. Baste in place.

2. Referring to the photograph on *page 59* for placement, arrange and baste the stem, flower, and leaf appliqués along the vines. (Marti layered and stitched together the multiple pieces of the

appliqué flowers before appliquéing the flowers to the foundation.)

3. Using threads in colors that match the fabrics, appliqué the shapes in place to complete a center panel.

4. Repeat steps 1 through 3 to appliqué a second red-and-green plaid 13½×84½" rectangle, completing a second center panel.

Assemble the Quilt Top

1. Referring to the photograph on *page 59*, lay out the three block rows, the two appliquéd center panels, and the two remaining red-and-green plaid 13½×84½" rectangles in vertical rows.

2. Sew together the rows. Press the seam allowances toward the red-and-green plaid rectangles. Trim the partial setting units in the block rows even with the red-and-green plaid rectangles.

3. Then add the red-and-green plaid 13½×84" rectangles to the top and bottom edges of the pieced rows to complete the quilt top. Press the seam allowances toward the red-and-green plaid rectangles.

Appliqué the Outer Panels

1. Intertwine the green print, burgundy print, and gold check ⅞"-wide vine strips on the outer red-and-green plaid panels as before; baste. Arrange the vine ends from the center panels amongst the vines on the outer panels; baste.

2. Referring to the photograph on *page 59*, arrange the remaining leaf appliqués along the vines on the outer panels and baste.

3. Using threads in colors that match the fabrics, appliqué the vines and leaves in place.

Complete the Quilt

1. Layer the quilt top, batting, and backing according to the instructions in Quilter's Schoolhouse, which begins on *page 150*. Quilt as desired.

2. Use the dark green print 2½×42" strips to bind the quilt according to the instructions in Quilter's Schoolhouse.

APPLIQUÉD TABLECLOTH

Embellish a festive tablecloth using fusible web, a leaf pattern, and simply cut bias-strip vines you meander along the border.

Materials

Scraps of assorted tan or ecru prints for appliqués

4—½-yard pieces of assorted beige prints for appliqués

Purchased 60×104" tablecloth

Rayon machine-embroidery thread

5 yards of lightweight fusible web

Cut the Fabrics

To make the best use of your fabrics, cut the pieces in the order that follows. *Note:* To make this project for an alternate tablecloth size, adjust the length of the appliqué vines and number of leaves as desired. This project uses "Texas Stars" leaf Pattern M, which is on *Pattern Sheet 2,* but you may choose to use leaf pattern L, or a combination of leaf shapes.

To use fusible web for appliquéing, as was done in this project, use the following steps.

1. Lay the fusible web, paper side up, over the pattern. With a pencil, trace the pattern 16 times, leaving ½" between tracings. Cut out each piece roughly ¼" outside the traced lines. Also cut eight 16" squares of fusible web.

2. Following the manufacturer's instructions, press the fusible-web Pattern M shapes onto the backs of the assorted tan and ecru print scraps; let cool. Cut out the pattern pieces on the drawn lines.

   Press two fusible-web 16" squares onto the backs of each beige print; let cool.

   Peel off the paper backings.

From assorted tan or ecru prints, cut:
• 16 of Pattern M

From *each* beige print, cut:
• 2—16" squares, cutting and piecing each set into enough ⅞"-wide bias strips to total 324" in length for vine appliqués (For more information on cutting bias strips, see Quilter's Schoolhouse, which begins on *page 150*). *Note:* Because of the fusible web, do not press seams open with a hot iron. Finger-press seams in one direction.

Appliqué the Tablecloth

1. Referring to the photograph *above* for placement ideas, intertwine the four vines in a free-form fashion on the tablecloth; position the 16 leaves as desired. Fuse in place.

2. Using matching thread and a machine satin stitch, appliqué the vines and leaves in place.

STAR BANNER

Accent a sunroom or an outdoor porch with this brightly colored banner made with

Texas Star blocks. Drape this small quilt across a dining room table, sofa table,

or kitchen island to welcome spring indoors.

Materials

¼ yard of gold print for blocks and inner border

⅓ yard of rose print for blocks

½ yard of green print for blocks and setting units

1¼ yards of blue print for setting units,
   outer border, and binding

1⅓ yards of backing fabric

22×48" of quilt batting

Finished quilt top: 15½×42"

Cut the Fabrics

To make the best use of your fabrics, cut the pieces in the order that follows. This project uses "Texas Stars" patterns A, B, C, and D on *Pattern Sheet 2.* To make templates of the patterns, follow the instructions in Quilter's Schoolhouse, which begins on *page 150.* The outer border and binding strips are cut the length of the fabric (parallel to the selvage). Extra length is added to allow for mitering the corners.

From gold print, cut:
• 4—1×42" strips for inner border
• 3 of Pattern A

From rose print, cut:
• 18 of Pattern B

From green print, cut:
• 18 of Pattern C
• 4 of Pattern D

From blue print, cut:
• 4—2½×42" binding strips
• 2—2½×42" outer border strips
• 4—2½×17" outer border strips
• 12 of Pattern D

Assemble the Texas Star Blocks

Referring to Assemble the Texas Star Blocks on *page 58,* use a gold print A hexagon, six rose print B pieces, and six green print C diamonds to make a Texas Star block. Repeat to make a total of three Texas Star blocks.

Assemble the Setting Units

Referring to Assemble the Setting Units instructions on *page 59,* use three blue print D triangles and one green print D triangle to make a triangle setting unit. Repeat to make a total of four triangle setting units.

Assemble the Quilt Center

Referring to the Quilt Assembly Diagram for placement, lay out the three Texas Star blocks and the four triangle setting units. Sew the units together to complete the quilt center. The pieced quilt center should measure 11×36½", including the seam allowances.

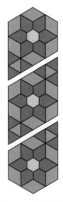

Quilt Assembly Diagram

Add the Borders

I. Cut the gold print 1×42" strips to make the following:
   • 2—1×39" inner border strips
   • 4—1×15" inner border strips

2. With midpoints and long edges aligned, join a gold print 1×39" inner border strip with a blue print 2½×42" outer border strip to make a long border strip set. Repeat to make a second long border strip set.

3. With midpoints and long edges aligned, join a gold print 1×15" inner border strip and a blue print 2½×17" outer border strip to make a short border strip set. Repeat to make a total of four short border strip sets.

4. With midpoints aligned, sew the long border strip sets to the long edges of the pieced quilt center and the short border strip sets to the angled edges of the pieced quilt center, beginning and ending the seams ¼" from the corners.

5. Miter the border corners to complete the quilt top. For information on mitering, see the instructions in Quilter's Schoolhouse, which begins on *page 150*.

Complete the Quilt

1. Layer the quilt top, batting, and backing according to the instructions in Quilter's Schoolhouse. Quilt as desired.

2. Use the blue print 2½×42" strips to bind the quilt according to the instructions in Quilter's Schoolhouse.

3. To hang, attach a hanging sleeve according to the instructions in Quilter's Schoolhouse about 5" from the top edge of the quilt. Slide a 20" long wooden dowel into the sleeve. Hot-glue finials and cording to each end of the dowel. Hang as desired.

BASKET
BEAUTIES

A favorite with quilt lovers, basket designs have appeared in all sizes and configurations for generations. Whether you prefer the pieced and scrappy charm of "Cottage Dreams," the patriotic appeal of "Baskets of Stars," or the appliquéd warmth of "Gathering Baskets," you'll fall in love all over again with this classic quilt motif. Stretch your boundaries: Experiment with unfamiliar color combinations or try a new technique. In no time at all, you'll have a basketful of memories.

Cottage
DREAMS

Although designer Lynn Dash chose to use just one fabric each for the

background, setting triangles, and border of this project, she selected more than

30 fabrics for the blocks to give the quilt a scrappy appearance.

Materials

2¾ yards of white print for blocks

1 yard of lavender print for setting triangles

1⅛ yards of green print for border

2 yards total of assorted pastel prints for blocks

½ yard total of assorted pink prints for binding

3½ yards of backing fabric

62×73" of quilt batting

Finished quilt top: 55×66⅜"
Finished blocks: 8" square

Quantities specified for 44/45"-wide, 100% cotton fabrics. All measurements include a ¼" seam allowance. Sew with right sides together unless otherwise stated.

Cut the Fabrics

To make the best use of your fabrics, cut the pieces in the order that follows. The following cutting instructions are for the block background, setting triangles, border, and binding pieces only. Instructions for cutting the assorted pastel prints accompany the block assembly instructions.

There are no pattern pieces for this project; the letter designations are for placement purposes only.

From white print, cut:
- 40—5½×2³⁄₁₆" rectangles for position E
- 10—5¼" squares, cutting each diagonally twice in an X for a total of 40 triangles for position A
- 12—4½" squares
- 10—3½" squares, cutting each in half diagonally for a total of 20 triangles for position G
- 30—2⅞" squares, cutting each in half diagonally for a total of 60 triangles for position C
- 40—2½" squares for position B
- 48—2½" squares
- 384—1½" squares

continued

From lavender print, cut:
- 4—12⅝" squares, cutting each diagonally twice in an X for a total of 16 setting triangles (you'll have 2 leftover triangles)
- 2—6⅝" squares, cutting each in half diagonally for a total of 4 corner triangles

From green print, cut:
- 6—5¼×42" strips for border

From assorted pink prints, cut:
- 6—2½×42" binding strips

Cut and Assemble the Basket Blocks

Cut the following pastel print pieces and follow steps 1 through 9 to complete one Basket block. Repeat the cutting and assembly steps to make a total of 20 blocks.

From pastel print No. 1, cut:
- 1—2½" square for position B
- 2—2⅞" squares, cutting each in half diagonally for a total of 4 triangles for position C (you'll have 1 leftover triangle)
- 1—2³⁄₁₆" square, cutting it in half diagonally for a total of 2 triangles for position F

From pastel print No. 2, cut:
- 1—6¼" square, cutting it in half diagonally for a total of 2 triangles for position D (you'll have 1 leftover triangle)

1. Sew together one pastel print C triangle and one white print C triangle to make a triangle-square (see Diagram 1). Press the seam allowance toward the pastel print triangle. The triangle-square should measure 2½" square, including the seam allowances.

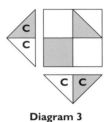

Diagram 1

2. Referring to Diagram 2 for placement, sew together the triangle-square, two white print B squares, and the pastel print B square in pairs. Press the seam allowances in opposite directions. Join the pairs. Press the seam allowance in one direction.

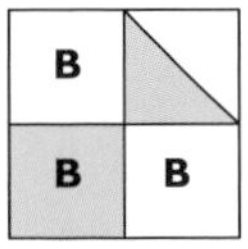

B | B
B | B

Diagram 2

3. Sew together a white print C triangle and a pastel print C triangle to make a triangle pair (see Diagram 3). Press the seam allowance toward the pastel print triangle. Repeat to make a second triangle pair that is a mirror image of the first.

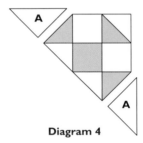

Diagram 3

4. Add the triangle pairs to the left-hand and bottom edges of the Step 2 unit. Press the seam allowances toward the Step 2 unit.

5. Referring to Diagram 4, sew a white print A triangle to opposite edges of the Step 4 unit to complete the basket top unit.

A

A

Diagram 4

6. Referring to Diagram 5, sew a pastel print F triangle to a white print E rectangle to make an E/F unit. Press the seam allowance toward the white print rectangle. Repeat to make a mirror-image E/F unit.

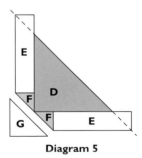

Diagram 5

7. Sew the E/F units to the short edges of a pastel print D triangle. Press the seam allowances toward the D triangle. Trim the white print E rectangles even with the raw edge of the pastel print D triangle.

8. Referring to Diagram 5 *opposite*, add a white print G triangle to the pastel print F triangles to make a basket base unit. Press the seam allowance toward the white print G triangle.

9. Sew together the basket top unit and the basket base unit to make a Basket block (see Diagram 6). Press the seam allowance toward the base unit. The pieced block should measure 8½" square, including the seam allowances.

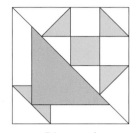

Diagram 6

Cut and Assemble the Flying Geese Blocks

Cut the following pastel print pieces and follow steps 1 through 6 to complete one Flying Geese block. Repeat the cutting and assembly steps to make a total of 12 blocks.

From pastel print No. 1, cut:
• 4—1½×2½" rectangles
From pastel print No. 2, cut:
• 4—1½×2½" rectangles
From pastel print No. 3, cut:
• 4—1½×2½" rectangles
From pastel print No. 4, cut:
• 4—1½×2½" rectangles

1. For accurate sewing lines, use a quilter's pencil to mark a diagonal line on the wrong side of each white print 1½" square. (To prevent your fabric from stretching as you draw the lines, place 220-grit sandpaper under the squares.)

2. Align a marked white print 1½" square with one end of a pastel print 1½×2½" rectangle (see Diagram 7; note the placement of the marked diagonal line). Stitch on the marked line; trim the excess fabric, leaving a ¼" seam allowance. Press the attached triangle open.

Diagram 7

3. In the same manner, align a second marked white print 1½" square with the opposite end of the same rectangle (see Diagram 7, again noting the placement of the marked diagonal line). Stitch on the marked line; trim and press as before to make a Flying Geese unit. The pieced Flying Geese unit should still measure 1½×2½", including the seam allowances.

4. Repeat steps 2 and 3 to make a total of four Flying Geese units from each pastel print.

5. Sew together four matching pastel print Flying Geese units to make a Flying Geese segment (see Diagram 8). Repeat with each of the remaining sets of Flying Geese units to make a total of four Flying Geese segments, each with a different print.

Diagram 8

continued

6. Referring to Diagram 9, join the four Flying Geese segments, four white print 2½" squares, and one white print 4½" square in three horizontal rows. Press the seam allowances toward the white print squares.

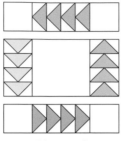

Diagram 9

Then join the rows to make a Flying Geese block. Press the seam allowances in one direction. The pieced block should measure 8½" square, including the seam allowances.

Assemble the Quilt Center

1. Referring to the photograph on *page 69* for placement, lay out the 20 Basket blocks, the 12 Flying Geese blocks, and the 14 lavender print setting triangles in diagonal rows.

2. Sew together the pieces in each row. Press the seam allowances toward the Flying Geese blocks and the setting triangles. Then join the rows. Press the seam allowances in one direction.

3. Add the lavender print corner triangles to complete the quilt center. Press the seam allowances toward the corner triangles.

Cottage Dreams Quilt
optional sizes

The pieced quilt center should measure 46×57⅜", including the seam allowances.

Add the Border

1. Cut and piece the green print 5¼×42" strips to make the following:
- 2—5¼×57⅜" border strips
- 2—5¼×55½" border strips

2. Sew the long green print border strips to the side edges of the pieced quilt center. Then join the short green print border strips to the top and bottom edges of the pieced quilt center to complete the quilt top. Press all seam allowances toward the border.

Complete the Quilt

1. Layer the quilt top, batting, and backing according to the instructions in Quilter's Schoolhouse, which begins on *page 150*.

2. Quilt as desired. In addition to machine-quilting in the ditch of each seam in each block, designer Lynn Dash quilted a simple motif in the white print center of each Flying Geese block and in the large pastel print triangle of each Basket block. She also machine-quilted an allover meandering pattern in the border.

3. Use the assorted pink print 2½×42" strips to bind the quilt according to the instructions in Quilter's Schoolhouse.

If you'd like to make this quilt in a size other than for a throw quilt, use the information *below*.

Alternate quilt sizes	Crib/Lap	Full/Queen	King
Number of Basket blocks	12	56	64
Number of Flying Geese blocks	6	42	49
Number of blocks wide by long	3×4	7×8	8×8
Finished size	43⅝×55"	89⅛×100½"	100½" square
Yardage requirements			
White print	1⅞ yards	6¾ yards	7¾ yards
Lavender print	⅔ yard	1⅓ yards	1⅝ yards
Green print	1 yard	1½ yards	1⅔ yards
Assorted pastel prints	⅔ yard total	4 yards total	4⅔ yards total
Assorted pink prints	½ yard total	⅞ yard total	⅞ yard total
Backing	2⅞ yards	8 yards	9 yards
Batting	50×61"	96×107"	107" square

MEMO QUILT

Fun fabrics in bright colors work together

to create a place to keep stamps, cards, pens,

or forget-me-not notes.

Materials

⅝ yard of white print for blocks and setting
  and corner triangles

¼ yard of purple print for inner border

⅝ yard of black floral for outer border

⅜ yard of multicolor stripe for binding

1 yard total of assorted bright prints in green,
  purple, orange, and black for blocks

1⅛ yards of backing fabric

38" square of quilt batting

Finished quilt top: 31¾" square

Cut the Fabrics

To make the best use of your fabrics, cut the pieces
in the order that follows. The following cutting
instructions are for the block background, setting
triangles, border, and binding pieces only.
Instructions for cutting the assorted bright prints
accompany the block assembly instructions. There
are no pattern pieces for this project; the letter
designations are for placement purposes only.

From white print, cut:
- 1—7⅝" square, cutting it diagonally twice in an X
  for a total of 4 large setting triangles
- 1—4½" square
- 2—3¾" squares, cutting each in half diagonally for
  a total of 4 corner triangles
- 8—2⅞" squares, cutting each in half diagonally for
  a total of 16 small setting triangles
- 8—2½" squares
- 128—1½" squares

From purple print, cut:
- 2—1×24¼" inner border strips
- 2—1×23¼" inner border strips

From black floral, cut:
- 2—4½×32¼" outer border strips
- 2—4½×24¼" outer border strips

From multicolor stripe, cut:
- 4—2½×42" binding strips

Cut and Assemble the Basket Blocks

Cut the assorted bright print pieces on *page 72*
and follow steps 1 through 3 to complete one
Basket block.

continued

From bright print No. 1, cut:

- 2—2⅞" squares, cutting each in half diagonally for a total of 4 triangles for position C (you'll have 1 leftover triangle)
- 1—2½" square for position B
- 1—2³⁄₁₆" square, cutting it in half diagonally for a total of 2 triangles for position F

From bright print No. 2, cut:

- 2—5½×2³⁄₁₆" rectangles for position E
- 1—5¼" square, cutting it diagonally twice in an X for a total of 4 triangles for position A (you'll have 2 leftover triangles)
- 2—2½" squares for position B
- 2—2⅞" squares, cutting each in half diagonally for a total of 4 triangles for position C (you'll have 1 leftover triangle)
- 1—3½" square, cutting it in half diagonally for a total of 2 triangles for position G (you'll have 1 leftover triangle)

From bright print No. 3, cut:

- 1—6¼" square, cutting it in half diagonally for a total of 2 triangles for position D (you'll have 1 leftover triangle)

- 1—6" square on the bias, folding it in half diagonally so the fold line is on the straight of grain for the pocket (see Diagram 1)

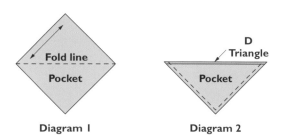

Diagram I   Diagram 2

1. Referring to Cut and Assemble the Basket Blocks on *page 68*, steps 1 to 5, use the bright print pieces to make a basket top unit.

2. Aligning raw edges, place the bright print No. 3 pocket piece atop a bright print No. 3 D triangle. The folded edge of the pocket piece should be at least ¼" away from the raw edge of the D triangle (see Diagram 2). Baste the raw edges together and treat the resulting D triangle and pocket as a single unit.

3. Referring to Cut and Assemble the Basket Blocks, steps 6 to 9, use the D triangle and pocket unit and the remaining bright print pieces to make a basket base unit and complete a Basket block.

4. Repeat steps 1 through 3 to make a total of four blocks.

Cut and Assemble the Flying Geese Blocks and Setting Pieces

From bright print No. 1, cut:
- 16—1½×2½" rectangles

From bright print No. 2, cut:
- 16—1½×2½" rectangles

From bright print No. 3, cut:
- 16—1½×2½" rectangles

From bright print No. 4, cut:
- 16—1½×2½" rectangles

1. Referring to Cut and Assemble the Flying Geese Blocks on *page 69*, steps 1 to 5, assemble 16 Flying Geese segments in sets of four from each color.

2. Referring to Step 6 on *page 70*, make one Flying Geese block.

3. Referring to Diagram 3 for placement, join two Flying Geese segments, one white print 2½" square, one white print large setting triangle, and two white print small setting triangles to make a pieced setting triangle. Press the seam allowances toward the square and setting triangles. Repeat to make a total of four pieced setting triangles.

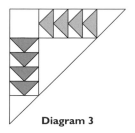 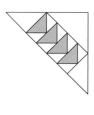

Diagram 3   **Diagram 4**

4. Referring to Diagram 4 for placement, join one Flying Geese segment, one white print corner triangle, and two small white print setting triangles to make a pieced corner triangle. Press the seam allowances toward the corner and

setting triangles. Repeat to make a total of four pieced corner triangles.

Assemble the Quilt Center

1. Referring to the photograph *opposite*, lay out the four Basket blocks, the Flying Geese block, and the four pieced setting triangles in diagonal rows.

2. Sew together the pieces in each row. Press the seam allowances toward the Flying Geese block and setting triangles. Join the rows. Press the seam allowances in one direction.

3. Add the pieced corner triangles to make the quilt center. Press the seam allowances in one direction. The pieced quilt center should measure 23¼" square, including the seam allowances.

Add the Borders

1. Sew the purple print 1×23¼" inner border strips to opposite edges of the quilt center. Then sew the purple print 1×24¼" inner border strips to the remaining edges of the quilt center. Press the seam allowances toward the border.

2. Sew the black floral 4½×24¼" outer border strips to opposite edges of the quilt top. Then sew the black floral 4½×32¼" outer border strips to the remaining edges of the quilt center to complete the quilt top. Press the seam allowances toward the outer border.

Complete the Quilt

1. Layer the quilt top, batting, and backing according to the instructions in Quilter's Schoolhouse, which begins on *page 150*. Quilt as desired.

2. Use the multicolor stripe 2½×42" strips to bind the quilt according to the instructions in Quilter's Schoolhouse.

3. Add a hanging sleeve on the back across the top edge according to the instructions in Quilter's Schoolhouse. To add weight and stability across the bottom, add a second sleeve and insert a slender piece of wood the same width as the sleeve.

Cottage Dreams

BED QUILT

Prints in cranberry and blue turn half

Basket blocks from "Cottage Dreams" into

a rich-looking quilt.

Materials

5⅝ yards of blue plaid for blocks, setting squares, inner border, and outer border

2⅜ yards of cranberry stripe for blocks, middle border, and binding

5⅓ yards of backing fabric

79×95" of quilt batting

Finished quilt top: 73×89"

Cut the Fabrics

To make the best use of your fabrics, cut the pieces in the order that follows. There are no pattern pieces for this project; the letter designations are for placement purposes only.

From blue plaid, cut:

- 8—5½×42" strips for outer border
- 7—2½×42" strips for inner border
- 31—8½" setting squares
- 96—2⅞" squares, cutting each in half diagonally for a total of 192 triangles for position C
- 256—2½" squares for position B

From cranberry stripe, cut:

- 1—27×42" rectangle, cutting it into enough 2½"-wide bias strips to total 334" in length (For specific instructions, see Cutting Bias Strips in Quilter's Schoolhouse, which begins on *page 150.*)
- 8—2×42" strips for middle border
- 96—2⅞" squares, cutting each in half diagonally for a total of 192 triangles for position C
- 64—2½" squares for position B

Assemble the Blocks

1. Sew together a blue plaid C triangle and a cranberry stripe C triangle to make a triangle-square (see Diagram 1, *page 68*). Press the seam allowance toward the blue plaid triangle. The triangle-square should measure 2½" square, including the seam allowances. Repeat to make a total of 192 triangle-squares.

2. Referring to Diagram 1, *opposite,* for placement, lay out six triangle-squares, eight blue plaid B squares, and two cranberry stripe B squares. Join

the pieces in each row. Press the seam allowances in one direction, alternating the direction with each row. Then join the rows to make a pieced block. Press the seam allowances in one direction. The pieced block should measure 8½" square, including the seam allowances. Repeat to make a total of 32 pieced blocks.

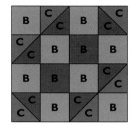

Diagram 1

Assemble the Quilt Center

1. Referring to the photograph *right* for placement, lay out the pieced blocks and the blue plaid 8½" setting squares in nine horizontal rows.

2. Sew together the blocks and setting squares in each row. Press the seam allowances toward the setting squares. Then join the rows to make the quilt center. Press the seam allowances in one direction. The pieced quilt center should measure 56½×72½", including the seam allowances.

Add the Borders

1. Cut and piece the blue plaid 2½×42" strips to make the following:
   • 2—2½×76½" inner border strips
   • 2—2½×56½" inner border strips

2. Sew the short inner border strips to the top and bottom edges of the quilt center. Then add the long inner border strips to each side edge of the quilt center. Press all seam allowances toward the inner border.

3. Cut and piece the cranberry stripe 2×42" strips to make the following:
   • 2—2×89½" middle border strips
   • 2—2×60½" middle border strips

4. Cut and piece the blue plaid 5½×42" strips to make the following:
   • 2—5½×89½" outer border strips
   • 2—5½×60½" outer border strips

5. Join one cranberry stripe 2×60½" border strip and one blue plaid 5½×60½" border strip to make a top border unit. Press the seam allowance toward the cranberry stripe strip. Repeat to make a bottom border unit. Sew the top and bottom border units to the top and bottom edges of the pieced quilt center with the cranberry stripe strip on the inside.

6. Join one cranberry stripe 2×89½" border strip and one blue plaid 5½×89½" border strip to make a side border unit. Press the seam allowance toward the cranberry stripe strip. Repeat to make a second side border unit. Sew the side border units to the side edges of the pieced quilt center with the cranberry stripe strip on the inside to complete the quilt top.

Complete the Quilt

1. Layer the quilt top, batting, and backing according to the instructions in Quilter's Schoolhouse, which begins on *page 150*. Quilt as desired.

2. Use the cranberry stripe 2½"-wide bias strips to bind the quilt according to the instructions in Quilter's Schoolhouse.

BASKETS OF
Stars

Careful planning allowed designer Darlene Zimmerman to piece each basket

from a different blue print. She used just two prints, either both blue or both

burgundy, to create each star block, putting the darker print in the center and

letting the lighter one compose the points.

Materials

1⅞ yards of white print for blocks, sashing,
   and border

1¼ yards total of assorted dark blue prints
   for blocks, sashing, border, and binding

⅜ yard total of assorted blue prints
   for blocks

½ yard total of assorted burgundy prints
   for blocks

1⅔ yards of backing fabric

46" square of quilt batting

Finished quilt top: 42" square
Finished four-basket block: 10" square
Finished five-star block: 10" square

Quantities specified for 44/45"-wide, 100% cotton fabrics. All measurements include a ¼" seam allowance. Sew with right sides together unless otherwise stated.

Cut the Fabrics

To make the best use of your fabrics, cut the pieces in the order that follows. The Basket Handle Pattern, the project's only pattern, is on *Pattern Sheet 1*; the letter designations are for placement purposes only. To make a template of the pattern, follow the instructions in Quilter's Schoolhouse, which begins on *page 150*.

continued

From white print, cut:
- 4—2½×34½" border strips
- 8—2½×9½" rectangles for position J
- 4—2½×8½" rectangles for position K
- 16—2½×3½" rectangles for position I
- 40—1½×3½" rectangles for position A
- 10—5⅞" squares, cutting each in half diagonally for a total of 20 triangles for position E
- 28—3¼" squares, cutting each diagonally twice in an X for a total of 112 triangles for position F
- 10—2⅞" squares, cutting each in half diagonally for a total of 20 triangles for position D
- 80—1½" squares for position G

From assorted dark blue prints, cut:
- 5—2½×42" binding strips (from same print)
- 8—1½×34½" border strips (from same print)
- 5—3⅞" squares, cutting each in half diagonally for a total of 10 triangles for position C
- 8—2½" squares for position H
- 42—1⅞" squares, cutting each in half diagonally for a total of 84 triangles for position B
- 10 of Basket Handle Pattern

From assorted blue prints, cut:
- 5—3⅞" squares, cutting each in half diagonally for a total of 10 triangles for position C
- 10 of Basket Handle Pattern
- 10—1⅞" squares, cutting each in half diagonally for a total of 20 triangles for position B

From assorted burgundy prints, cut:
- 20—2½" squares for position H
- 80—1⅞" squares, cutting each in half diagonally for a total of 160 triangles for position B

Assemble the Basket Blocks

1. For one Basket block you'll need two white print A rectangles, two blue print B triangles, one blue print C triangle, one white print D triangle, one white print E triangle, and one blue print basket handle piece.

2. Referring to Diagram 1 for placement, sew the blue print B triangles to the white print A rectangles to make two A/B units that are mirror images of each other. Press the seam allowances toward the white print rectangles.

Diagram 1

3. Sew the A/B units to the short edges of the blue print C triangle (see Diagram 2). Press the seam allowances toward the C triangle.

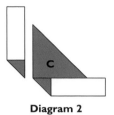

Diagram 2

4. Referring to Diagram 3, add the white print D triangle to the A/B/C unit. Press the seam allowance toward the white print D triangle. Trim the white print A rectangles even with the raw edge of the blue print C triangle to make a basket base unit.

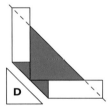

Diagram 3

5. Center the blue print basket handle piece along the long edge of the white print E triangle (see Diagram 4). Using blue thread, appliqué the handle in place to make the basket handle unit.

Diagram 4

6. Aligning long edges, sew together the basket base and basket handle units to make a blue Basket block. Press the seam allowance toward the basket base. The pieced block should measure 5½" square, including the seam allowances.

7. Repeat steps 1 through 6 to make a total of 10 blue Basket blocks. Then repeat steps 1 through 6 using the dark blue print pieces in place of the blue print pieces to make a total of 10 dark blue Basket blocks.

Assemble the Four-Basket Blocks

I. Referring to the photograph on *page 77* for placement, lay out four Basket blocks in a square.

2. Sew the blocks together in pairs. Press the seam allowances in opposite directions. Then join the pairs to make a four-basket block. Press the seam allowance in one direction. The pieced four-basket block should measure 10½" square, including the seam allowances.

3. Repeat steps 1 and 2 to make a total of five four-basket blocks.

Assemble the Five-Star Blocks

I. Referring to Diagram 5 for placement, sew two burgundy print B triangles to a white print F triangle to make a burgundy Flying Geese unit. Press the seam allowances toward the burgundy print triangles. The pieced Flying Geese unit should measure 1½×2½", including the seam allowances. Repeat using two dark blue print B triangles and one white print F triangle to make a dark blue Flying Geese unit.

Diagram 5

2. Repeat Step 1 to make a total of 80 burgundy Flying Geese units and 32 dark blue Flying Geese units. Set aside 16 dark blue Flying Geese units for the sashing.

3. Sew a dark blue Flying Geese unit to a short edge of a white print I rectangle to make a star point unit (see Diagram 6). Press the seam allowance toward the white print I rectangle. Repeat to make a total of 16 star point units.

Diagram 6

4. Referring to Diagram 7, lay out four burgundy Flying Geese units, four white print G squares, and one burgundy print H square in three horizontal rows. Sew together the pieces in each row. Press the seam allowances toward the white

print G squares or the burgundy print H square. Then join the rows to make an Ohio Star block. Press the seam allowances in one direction. The pieced Ohio Star block should measure 4½" square, including the seam allowances.

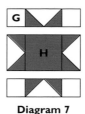

Diagram 7

5. Repeat Step 4 to make a total of 20 Ohio Star blocks. Set aside four blocks for the border.

6. Referring to Diagram 8, lay out four Ohio Star blocks, four star point units, and one dark blue print H square in three horizontal rows. Sew together the pieces in each row. Press the seam allowances toward the star point units. Then join the rows to make a five-star block. Press the seam allowances in one direction. The pieced five-star block should measure 10½" square, including the seam allowances.

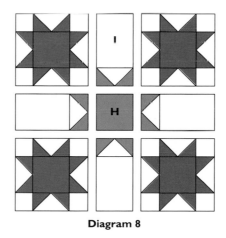

Diagram 8

7. Repeat Step 6 to make a total of four five-star blocks.

Assemble the Sashing

I. Sew a dark blue Flying Geese unit to a short edge of a white print J rectangle to make a Sashing Unit A (see Diagram 9 on *page 80*). Press the seam allowance toward the white print rectangle. Repeat to make a total of eight of Sashing Unit A.

continued

2. Sew a dark blue Flying Geese unit to each short edge of a white print K rectangle to make a Sashing Unit B (see Diagram 10). Press the seam allowances toward the white print rectangle. Repeat to make a total of four of Sashing Unit B.

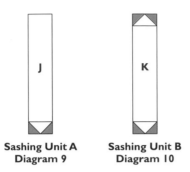

Sashing Unit A
Diagram 9

Sashing Unit B
Diagram 10

Assemble the Quilt Center

1. Referring to the photograph on *page 77*, lay out the four-basket blocks, the five-star blocks, sashing units A and B, and the remaining four dark blue print H squares in five horizontal rows.

2. Sew together the pieces in each row. Press the seam allowances toward the sashing units.

3. Join the rows to make the quilt center. Press the seam allowances in one direction. The pieced quilt center should measure 34½" square, including the seam allowances.

Assemble and Add the Border

1. Aligning long edges, sew together two dark blue print 1½×34½" strips and one white print 2½×34½" strip to make a pieced border unit. Press the seam allowances toward the dark blue print strips. Repeat to make a total of four pieced border units.

2. Sew a pieced border unit to opposite edges of the pieced quilt center. Press the seam allowances toward the border.

3. Add a remaining Ohio Star block to each end of the remaining pieced border units. Press the seam allowances toward the border strips. Then add the pieced border units to the remaining edges of the pieced quilt center to complete the quilt top. Press the seam allowances toward the border.

Complete the Quilt

1. Layer the quilt top, batting, and backing according to the instructions in Quilter's Schoolhouse, which begins on *page 150*. Quilt as desired.

2. Use the dark blue print 2½×42" strips to bind the quilt according to the instructions in Quilter's Schoolhouse.

Baskets of Stars Quilt

optional sizes

If you'd like to make this quilt in a size other than for a wall hanging, use the information *below*.

Alternate quilt sizes	Throw	Twin	Full/Queen
Basket blocks	52	72	100
Ohio Star blocks	52	72	100
Number of four-basket blocks	13	18	25
Number of five-star blocks	12	17	24
Number of blocks wide by long	5×5	5×7	7×7
Finished size	66" square	66×90"	90" square
Yardage requirements			
White print	3½ yards	5⅛ yards	6½ yards
Assorted dark blue prints	2 yards	2⅝ yards	3⅓ yards
Assorted blue prints	⅔ yard	¾ yard	1⅛ yards
Assorted burgundy prints	1 yard	1¼ yards	1⅔ yards
Backing	4 yards	5⅓ yards	8 yards
Batting	72" square	72×96"	96" square

BED QUILT

Showcasing reproduction 1880s fabrics,
this antique-looking quilt sets a scrappy tone
using a variety of prints in the stars.

Materials

1¾ yards total of assorted dark prints in
  red, green, orange, yellow, brown, and blue
  for blocks

1¾ yards total of assorted blue prints for
  blocks, sashing, and border

3¼ yards total of assorted pink prints for blocks

2½ yards of light pink print for sashing, border,
  and binding

5⅛ yards of backing fabric

68×92" of quilt batting

Finished quilt top: 62×86"

Cut the Fabrics

To make the best use of your fabrics, cut the pieces
in the order that follows. *Note:* Each five-star block
contains one set of matching pink prints.

There are no pattern pieces for this project; the
letter designations are for placement purposes only.

From assorted dark prints, cut:
• 288—1⅞" squares, cutting each in half diagonally
  for a total of 576 triangles for position B (72 sets
  of 8)
• 90—2½" squares for position H
• 144—1½" squares for position A (18 sets of 8)

From assorted blue prints, cut:
• 272—1⅞" squares, cutting each in half diagonally
  for a total of 544 triangles for position B (68 sets
  of 8)

• 85—2½" squares for position H
• 28—2½" squares for sashing and border
• 136—1½" squares for position A (17 sets of 8)

From assorted pink prints, cut:
• 140—3¼" squares, cutting each diagonally twice
  in an X for a total of 560 triangles for position F
  (35 sets of 16)
• 140—2½×4½" rectangles for position I
  (35 sets of 4)
• 560—1½" squares for position G (35 sets of 16)

From light pink print, cut:
• 7—2½×42" strips for border
• 8—2½×42" binding strips
• 58—2½×10½" rectangles for sashing

continued

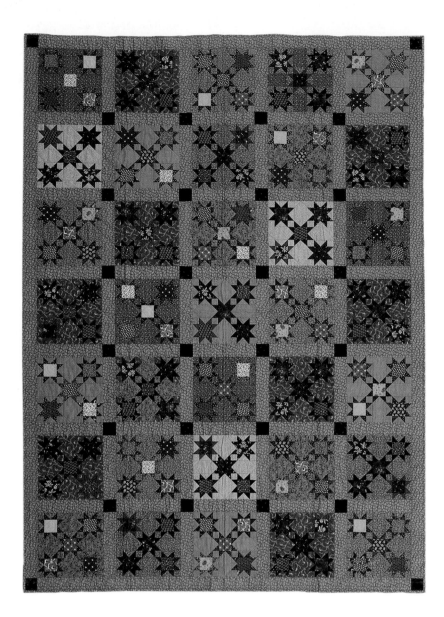

Baskets of Stars

Assemble the Five-Star Blocks

1. To make a dark print five-star block, you'll need four sets of eight matching dark print B triangles, five dark print H squares, eight matching dark print A squares, and the following pieces in the same pink print: 16 F triangles, 16 G squares, and four I rectangles.

2. Referring to Assemble the Five-Star Blocks on *page 79*, Step 1, sew two dark print B triangles to a pink print F triangle to make a Flying Geese unit; press. Repeat to make a total of 16 dark print Flying Geese units.

3. Referring to Diagram 7 on *page 79*, lay out four matching Flying Geese units, four pink print G squares, and one dark print H square in three

horizontal rows. Sew together the pieces in each row; press. Then join the rows to make an Ohio Star block. Press the seam allowances in one direction. Repeat to make a total of four Ohio Star blocks.

4. Draw a diagonal line on the wrong side of the eight dark print A squares.

5. Align a marked dark print A square on one corner of a pink print I rectangle (see Diagram 1, noting the direction of the drawn diagonal line). Stitch on the drawn line. Trim the seam allowance to ¼" and press the attached triangle open.

  Repeat with a second marked dark print A square on the adjacent corner of the rectangle, again noting the direction of the drawn line in Diagram 1. Stitch, trim, and press as before to make a star point unit. Repeat to make four star point units.

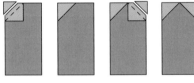

Diagram 1

6. Referring to Diagram 2, lay out the four Ohio Star blocks, the four star point units, and the remaining dark print H square in three horizontal rows. Sew together the pieces in each row; press the seam allowances toward the star point units. Then join the rows to make a five-star block; press the seam allowances in one direction.

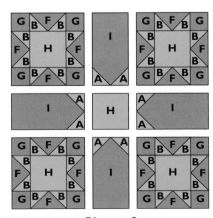

Diagram 2

7. Repeat steps 1 through 6 to make a total of 18 dark print five-star blocks.

8. Repeat steps 1 through 6 using assorted blue print pieces in place of the dark print ones to make a total of 17 blue print five-star blocks.

Assemble the Quilt Center

1. Referring to the photograph *opposite*, lay out the dark print and blue print five-star blocks, the light pink print 2½×10½" sashing rectangles, and the blue print 2½" sashing squares in 13 horizontal rows.

2. Sew together the pieces in each row; press the seam allowances toward the sashing pieces.

3. Join the rows to make the quilt center; press the seam allowances in one direction. The pieced quilt center should measure 58½×82½", including the seam allowances.

Add the Border

1. Cut and piece the light pink print 2½×42" strips to make the following:
  • 2—2½×82½" border strips
  • 2—2½×58½" border strips

2. Sew the long border strips to the side edges of the quilt center. Press the seam allowances toward the border.

3. Sew one assorted blue print 2½" square to each end of the short border strips to make two border units. Each border unit should measure 2½×62½", including the seam allowances. Press the seam allowances toward the blue print. Then join a border unit to the top and bottom edges of the quilt center to complete the quilt top. Press the seam allowances toward the border.

Complete the Quilt

1. Layer the quilt top, batting, and backing according to the instructions in Quilter's Schoolhouse, which begins on *page 150*. Quilt as desired.

2. Use the light pink print 2½×42" strips to bind the quilt according to the instructions in Quilter's Schoolhouse.

TOKEN QUILTS

These small quilts make cherished gifts.

Materials for Token Quilt I

8×16" rectangle of red print for basket block and corner triangles

8×12" rectangle of beige print for basket block

⅛ yard of solid brown for border

4—2½×12" strips of assorted prints for pieced binding

13" square of backing fabric

13" square of quilt batting

4" square of lightweight fusible web

45 assorted white buttons

Permanent fine-line fabric pen: brown

Finished quilt tops: 9" square

continued

Token Quilt I

Cut the Fabrics

To make the best use of your fabrics, cut the pieces in the order that follows. The project uses only the "Baskets of Stars" Basket Handle Pattern on *Pattern Sheet 1*. The letter designations are for placement purposes only.

To use fusible web for appliquéing, as was done in this project, complete the following steps.

1. Lay the fusible web, paper side up, over the Basket Handle pattern. With a pencil, trace the pattern once. Cut out the fusible web piece roughly ¼" outside the traced lines.

2. Following the manufacturer's instructions, press the fusible-web piece onto the back of the red print; let cool. Cut out the fabric piece on the drawn lines. Peel off the paper backing.

From red print, cut:
- 2—4½" squares, cutting each in half diagonally for a total of 4 corner triangles
- 1—3⅞" square, cutting it in half diagonally for a total of 2 triangles for position C (you'll have 1 leftover triangle)
- 1—1⅞" square, cutting it in half diagonally for a total of 2 triangles for position B

From beige print, cut:
- 1—5⅞" square, cutting it in half diagonally for a total of 2 triangles for position E (you'll have 1 leftover triangle)
- 1—2⅞" square, cutting it in half diagonally for a total of 2 triangles for position D (you'll have 1 leftover triangle)
- 2—1½×3½" rectangles for position A

From solid brown, cut:
- 2—1½×9½" border strips
- 2—1½×7½" border strips

Assemble the Quilt Center

1. Referring to Assemble the Basket Blocks on *page 78*, use the beige print A rectangles, red print B triangles, red print C triangle, beige print D triangle, beige print E triangle, and the red print basket handle to make a Basket Block. Fuse the basket handle in place, rather than using hand appliqué, before joining the basket base and basket handle units.

2. Sew two red print corner triangles to opposite edges of the Basket block. Then add the remaining red print corner triangles to the remaining edges of the Basket block to make the quilt center. Trim the pieced quilt center to measure 7½" square, including seam allowances.

Add the Border

Sew the solid brown 1½×7½" border strips to opposite edges of the quilt center. Then sew the solid brown 1½×9½" border strips to the remaining edges of the quilt center to complete the quilt top. Press the seam allowances toward the border.

Complete the Quilt

1. Using the permanent fabric pen, lightly draw shading lines on the basket handle and base.

2. Layer the quilt top, batting, and backing according to the instructions in Quilter's Schoolhouse. Quilt as desired.

3. Use the assorted print 2½×12" strips to bind the quilt according to the instructions in Quilter's Schoolhouse.

4. Sew the assorted white buttons onto the quilt as shown in the photograph *above*.

Materials for Token Quilt II

9½" square of tan felted wool for appliqué
   foundation

8" square of white felted wool for basket and
   circle appliqués

5" square of red felted wool for circle appliqués

4—2½×12" strips of assorted prints for
   pieced binding

13" square of backing fabric

13" square of quilt batting

5" square of lightweight fusible web

9 assorted white buttons

4 assorted red buttons

Embroidery floss: red and white

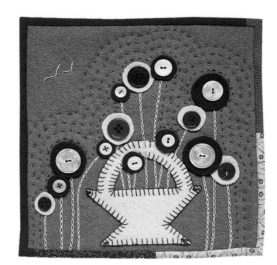

Token Quilt II

Cut the Fabrics

See the fusing instructions under Cut the Fabrics, *opposite,* but use the Token Quilt II Basket Pattern on *Pattern Sheet 1* and white wool instead of the Basket Handle Pattern and red print.

From white felted wool, cut:
• 4 backing circles for red buttons, making the circles slightly bigger in diameter than the buttons

From red felted wool, cut:
• 9 backing circles for red buttons, making the circles slightly bigger in diameter than the buttons

Assemble the Quilt Top

1. Position the white wool basket piece on the tan 9½" square wool appliqué foundation and fuse in place. Using two strands of red embroidery floss, blanket-stitch around the basket.

   To blanket-stitch, pull your needle up at A, form a reverse L shape with the floss, and hold the angle of the L shape in place with your thumb. Push the needle down at B and come up at C to secure the stitch.

Blanket Stitch

2. Using two strands of white embroidery floss, chain-stitch the flower stems and backstitch the birds.

   To chain-stitch, pull your needle up at A, form a U shape with the floss, and hold the shape in place with your thumb. Push your needle down at B, about ⅛" from A, and come up at C.

Chain Stitch

   To backstitch, pull your needle up at A. Insert it back into the fabric at B, and bring it up at C. Push your needle down again at D, and bring it up at E.

Backstitch

3. Place each button atop an opposite-color wool circle. Using red embroidery floss, stitch the button units to the foundation atop the stems.

Complete the Quilt

1. Layer the quilt top, batting, and backing according to the instructions in Quilter's Schoolhouse. Quilt as desired.

2. Use the assorted print 2½×12" strips to bind the quilt according to the instructions in Quilter's Schoolhouse.

GATHERING *Baskets*

From one pattern, Florida designers Cindy Blackberg and Mary Sorensen created

two stunning quilts that will challenge your piecing and appliquéing skills.

Materials

1 yard of cream print for blocks and outer border

4—¼-yard pieces of assorted green prints for blocks

16—2×6½" pieces of assorted dark red prints for blocks

32—2×6½" pieces of assorted blue prints for blocks

16—2×6½" pieces of assorted dark gold prints for blocks

½ yard of tan print for blocks and appliqué foundations

18×22" piece (fat quarter) of brown print for appliqués

Scraps of assorted gold, green, red, purple, dark peach, dark red, and blue prints for appliqués and pieced border

½ yard of dark green print for pieced border

⅜ yard of dark gold print for binding

2⅞ yards of backing fabric

51" square of quilt batting

Embroidery floss: brown and green

Finished quilt top: 45" square
Finished large Basket block: 10⅝" square
Finished small Basket block: 6" square

Quantities specified for 44/45"-wide, 100% cotton fabrics. All measurements include a ¼" seam allowance. Sew with right sides together unless otherwise stated.

Designer Notes

Cindy Blackberg likes to piece. Mary Sorensen likes to appliqué. Both enjoy hand quilting. Frequently they work together, making two quilts from the same pattern.

The instructions here are specific to Cindy's version, shown in the foreground in the photograph *opposite*. Mary's version is in the background of the photograph *opposite* and on *page 90*.

continued

Cut the Fabrics

To make the best use of your fabrics, cut the pieces in the order that follows. The patterns are on *Pattern Sheet 1*. To make templates of the patterns, follow the instructions in Quilter's Schoolhouse, which begins on *page 150.*

From cream print, cut:
- 4—6½×33½" outer border strips
- 4 *each* of patterns D and F
- 8 *each* of patterns E and G

From *each* assorted green print, cut:
- 1 *each* of patterns B and BB
- 2 *each* of patterns C and CC

From *each* assorted dark red print, cut:
- 1 *each* of patterns A and AA

From *each* assorted blue print, cut:
- 1 *each* of patterns A and AA

From *each* assorted dark gold print, cut:
- 1 *each* of patterns A and AA

From tan print, cut:
- 2—18" squares for appliqué foundations (You'll cut them into triangles after you've completed the appliqué.)
- 4 *each* of patterns DD and FF
- 8 *each* of patterns EE and GG

From brown print, cut:
- 1—18" square, cutting it into enough ⅝"-wide bias strips to total 24" in length (For specific instructions, see Cutting Bias Strips in Quilter's Schoolhouse, which begins on *page 150.*)

From gold print scraps, cut:
- 84 of Pattern H
- 2 *each* of patterns 1 and 2
- 70 of Pattern 6

From green print scraps, cut:
- 1 *each* of patterns 3, 5 reversed, 11, 12, 12 reversed, 14, and 14 reversed
- 2 of Pattern 3 reversed
- 3 *each* of patterns 4, 4 reversed, 5, and 15 reversed
- 4 *each* of patterns 15 and 20 reversed
- 5 *each* of patterns 8 and 8 reversed
- 12 of Pattern 20

From red print scraps, cut:
- 2 *each* of patterns 13 and 19
- 9 of Pattern 21

From purple print scraps, cut:
- 7 of Pattern 21
- 4 of Pattern 22

From dark peach print scraps, cut:
- 2 *each* of patterns 9 and 10

From dark red print scraps, cut:
- 3 *each* of patterns 16 and 17
- 2 of Pattern 18

From blue print scraps, cut:
- 14 of Pattern 7

From dark green print, cut:
- 160 of Pattern J
- 16 of Pattern K

From dark gold print, cut:
- 5—2½×42" binding strips

Assemble the Large Basket Blocks

1. For one large Basket block you'll need four dark red print A diamonds, eight blue print A diamonds, four dark gold print A diamonds, one green print B triangle, two green print C triangles, one cream print D square, two cream print E triangles, one cream print F triangle, and two cream print G rectangles.

2. Lay out one dark red print A diamond, two blue print A diamonds, and one dark gold print A diamond as shown in Diagram 1. Sew together the diamonds in pairs. Press the seam allowances in opposite directions. Then join the pairs to make a diamond point. Press the seam allowance in one direction. Repeat to make a total of four diamond points.

Diagram I   **Diagram 2**

3. Referring to Diagram 2 for placement, sew together the four diamond points, beginning and ending at the ¼" seam allowances.

4. Referring to Diagram 3, *opposite,* set in the cream print E triangles and the cream print D square to make a basket top unit. (For specific instructions on setting in seams, see Quilter's Schoolhouse, which begins on *page 150.*)

5. Sew the green print B triangle to the bottom edge of the basket top unit. Then add a green print C triangle to one end of each cream print G rectangle; join to the basket top unit. Add the cream print F triangle to complete a large

Basket block. The pieced large Basket block should measure 11⅛" square, including the seam allowances.

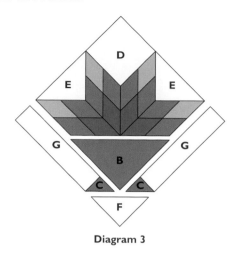

Diagram 3

6. Repeat steps 1 through 5 to make a total of four large Basket blocks.

Assemble the Small Basket Blocks

1. For one small Basket block you'll need four dark red print AA diamonds, eight blue print AA diamonds, four dark gold print AA diamonds, one green print BB triangle, two green print CC triangles, one tan print DD square, two tan print EE triangles, one tan print FF triangle, and two tan print GG rectangles.

2. Sew the pieces together in the same order as the large Basket block to make a small Basket block. The pieced small Basket block should measure 6½" square, including the seam allowances. Repeat to make a total of four small Basket blocks.

Appliqué the Setting Triangles

1. Prepare the appliqué pieces and bias strips for stems by basting under the ³⁄₁₆" seam allowances. (For specific information on appliqué, see Quilter's Schoolhouse, which begins on *page 150*.)

2. Using a quilter's pencil, draw a diagonal line on the wrong side of each tan print 18" square appliqué foundation. Referring to the four different appliqué placement diagrams on *Pattern Sheet 1*, lay out the appliqué pieces for two setting triangles on each square foundation. Baste in place.

3. For the stems, cut the bias strips into the lengths needed. Position the stems on the foundations according to the placement diagrams. Baste.

4. Using small slip stitches and threads in colors that match the fabrics, appliqué the pieces to the foundations. Work from the bottom appliqué piece to the top. Remove basting thread.

5. Using a stem stitch and two strands of green embroidery floss, embroider the cherry stems as shown on the placement diagrams. Using two strands of brown embroidery floss, stem-stitch the fruit tendrils.

To stem-stitch, pull your needle up at A, then insert it back into the fabric at B, about ³⁄₈" away from A. Holding the floss out of the way, bring your needle back up at C and pull the floss through so it lies flat against the fabric. The distances between points A, B, and C should be equal. Pull with equal tautness after each stitch.

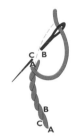

Stem Stitch

6. Trim the appliquéd foundations to measure 15⅞" square, then cut each foundation in half diagonally to make four appliquéd setting triangles.

Assemble the Quilt Center

1. Referring to the foreground quilt in the photograph on *page 86* for placement, sew together the pieced large Basket blocks in pairs. Press the seam allowances in opposite directions. Then join the pairs to make the center square. Press the seam allowance in one direction.

2. Lay out the remaining appliqué pieces on the pieced center square.

3. Using small slip stitches and threads in colors that match the fabrics, appliqué the pieces to the pieced center square.

4. Sew an appliquéd setting triangle to opposite edges of the pieced center square. Then sew the remaining two appliquéd setting triangles to the remaining raw edges to make the quilt center.

continued

The pieced quilt center should measure 30½" square, including the seam allowances.

Assemble and Add the Pieced Border

1. Sew dark green print J triangles to opposite edges of 76 gold print H squares to make a total of 76 of border unit 1 (see Diagram 4). Press the seam allowances toward the dark green print triangles.

Diagram 4

Diagram 5

2. Referring to Diagram 5, join a dark green print J triangle and a dark green print K triangle to opposite edges of eight gold print H squares to make a block subunit. Press the seam allowances toward the dark green print triangles. Sew a second dark green print K triangle to each pieced subunit to make a total of eight of border unit 2. Press the seam allowances toward the dark green print triangles.

3. Matching seams, join 18 of border unit 1 and two of border unit 2 to make a short pieced border strip (see Diagram 6). Press the seam allowances in one direction. The short pieced border strip should measure 2×30½", including the seam allowances. Repeat to make a second short pieced border strip.

Diagram 6

4. Sew the short pieced border strips to opposite edges of the pieced quilt center. Press the seam allowances toward the pieced border.

5. Matching seams, join 20 of border unit 1 and two of border unit 2 to make a long pieced border strip. Press the seam allowances in one direction. The long pieced border strip should measure 2×33½", including the seam allowances. Repeat to make a second long pieced border strip.

6. Sew the long pieced border strips to the remaining edges of the pieced quilt center. Press the seam allowances toward the pieced border.

Add the Outer Border

1. Sew a cream print 6½×33½" outer border strip to opposite edges of the pieced quilt center.

2. Sew a small Basket block to each end of the remaining cream print 6½×33½" outer border strips. Add the pieced border strips to the remaining edges of the pieced quilt center to complete the quilt top. Press all seam allowances toward the outer border.

optional colors

Mary Sorensen chose a darker palette than Cindy Blackberg for her vibrant version of "Gathering Baskets." She combined gold prints with dark gold and dark red prints to create a warm, autumnal wall hanging. She added black prints for deep contrast. The wide outer border showcases her hand-quilted parallel lines.

Gathering Baskets

Complete the Quilt

1. Layer the quilt top, batting, and backing according to the instructions in Quilter's Schoolhouse, which begins on *page 150.*

2. Quilt as desired. Cindy hand-quilted her quilt center using a ½"-wide diagonal grid.

3. Use the dark gold print 2½×42" strips to bind the quilt according to the instructions in Quilter's Schoolhouse.

APPLIQUÉD BREAD COVER

With fusible web and your sewing machine, colorful flowers can blossom on a piece of prairie cloth for a quick-and-easy gift.

Materials

Scraps of assorted yellow, pink, lavender, and green prints for appliqués

24" square of beige prairie cloth or 28-count Aida cloth for appliqué foundation

Lightweight fusible web

Three assorted buttons

Cut the Fabrics

To make the best use of your fabrics, cut the pieces in the order that follows.

This project uses "Gathering Baskets" patterns 6 and 8, which are on *Pattern Sheet 1.* To use fusible web for appliquéing, as was done in this project, complete the following steps.

1. Lay the fusible web, paper side up, over patterns 6 and 8. With a pencil, trace each pattern the number of times specified in Step 2, leaving ½" between tracings. Cut out the fusible-web pieces roughly ¼" outside the traced lines.

2. Following the manufacturer's instructions, press the fusible-web pieces onto the backs of the designated fabrics; let cool. Cut out the fabric pieces on the drawn lines. Peel off the paper backings.

From assorted yellow, pink, and lavender prints, cut:
• 5 *each* of Pattern 6
From assorted green prints, cut:
• 4 *each* of patterns 8 and 8 reversed

Appliqué the Bread Cover

1. Sew a straight or zigzag stitch ½" from the edges of the 24"-square appliqué foundation. Remove threads to fray the edges to the stitching lines.

2. Referring to the photograph *above,* position the appliqué pieces on the foundation. Fuse the appliqués in place.

3. Using matching machine-embroidery thread, machine-satin-stitch around each appliqué piece.

4. Stitch a button in the center of each flower.

FRAMED ART

Machine appliqué and a combination of prints, batiks, and hand-dyed fabrics form this picture-perfect work of art.

Materials

½ yard of dark green print for appliqué foundation and binding

Scraps of assorted brown, gold, green, peach, dark peach, red, and purple prints for appliqués

18×24" of backing fabric

18×24" of quilt batting

1 yard of lightweight fusible web

Machine-embroidery thread (40-weight rayon or 50-weight cotton thread) in matching and accenting colors for appliqué

Finished quilt top: 13×17"

Cut the Fabrics

To make the best use of your fabrics, cut the pieces in the order that follows.

This project uses some of the "Gathering Baskets" patterns, which are on *Pattern Sheet 1*. To use fusible web for appliquéing, as was done in this project, complete the following steps.

1. Lay the fusible web, paper side up, over the patterns listed in Step 2 *below*. With a pencil, trace each pattern the number of times specified, leaving ½" between tracings. Cut out the fusible-web pieces roughly ¼" outside the traced lines. Cut ¼" inside the traced lines of each fusible-web piece and discard the centers.

2. Following the manufacturer's instructions, press the fusible-web pieces onto the backs of the designated fabrics; let cool. Cut out the fabric pieces on the drawn lines. Peel off the paper backings.

From dark green print cut:
• 2—1½×42" binding strips
• 1—14×18" rectangle for appliqué foundation

From assorted brown prints, cut:
• 1 of Pattern B, including seam allowances (extend the seam allowance to points)
• 2 of Pattern C, including seam allowances (extend the seam allowance to points)

From assorted gold prints, cut:
- 2 of Pattern 1 reversed

From assorted green prints, cut:
- 3 of Pattern 13
- 2 of Pattern 2 reversed
- 1 *each* of patterns 3, 3 reversed, 4, and 4 reversed

From assorted peach prints, cut:
- 2 of Pattern 9 reversed

From assorted dark peach prints, cut:
- 2 of Pattern 10 reversed

From assorted red prints, cut:
- 5 of Pattern 21
- 2 of Pattern 19
- 1 of Pattern 18

From assorted purple prints, cut:
- 17 of Pattern 21
- 6 of Pattern 22
- 2 of Pattern 16 reversed
- 2 of Pattern 17 reversed

Appliqué the Foundation

I. Referring to the photograph *right*, arrange all of the appliqué pieces on the dark green print 14×18" rectangle foundation, first placing basket pieces B and C about 2½" above the foundation's bottom edge. When you are pleased with the arrangement, fuse the pears, peaches, and plums to the foundation.

2. Using a 1.5-mm-wide, .75-mm-long zigzag stitch and matching threads, stitch around the edges of each appliqué.

3. Using a straight stitch and green thread, stitch a vein line in each leaf. Using light gray-brown thread and a 3-mm-wide satin stitch, make a ½"-long stem on each pear. Using bright green thread and a machine-set football-shape satin-stitch pattern, stitch five or six leaves on the top of each strawberry.

4. Using a machine-set triple stitch and dark green thread, stitch stems on the cherries.

Complete the Quilt

I. Layer the appliquéd foundation, batting and backing according to the instructions in Quilter's Schoolhouse, which begins on *page 150*.

2. Using monofilament thread, quilt around each appliqué piece and on the leaf veins. Use brown thread to quilt a basket-weave design on the brown print basket. Use green thread to quilt diagonal lines in both directions on the background.

3. Trim the quilt to 13½×17½".

4. The binding on this quilt only shows on the back. Follow the instructions in Quilter's Schoolhouse to prepare the dark green print 1½×42" strips for binding. Stitch the prepared binding strips to the quilt top with a ¼" seam allowance, pivoting at the corners instead of making a mitered fold. Fold the entire width of the binding to the back, so the binding seam line becomes the quilt's edge; stitch the binding to the back by hand.

5. Mat and frame as desired.

ROTARY-CUT
CREATIONS

Accurately cut pieces mean even a beginning quiltmaker can assemble a quilt with ease, and a rotary cutter can go a long way toward making that possible. Any of these projects—the floral garden of "Abby's Wish," the bright colors of "Brilliant Trip Around the World," or the pastel palette of "Heaven's Stairway"—will give you an opportunity to perfect your rotary-cutting skills and stretch your creativity as a quilter.

ABBY'S *Wish*

In this bold double-bed-size quilt, a garden maze setting surrounds 18 stars,

each composed of assorted red and green prints.

Materials

18—9×22" pieces (fat eighths) of assorted red and
  green prints for blocks

2 yards of cream print for blocks

1⅓ yards of dark red print for blocks

1¼ yards of solid red for sashing

1½ yards of solid green for sashing and
  inner border

4½ yards of red floral for sashing, setting triangles,
  outer border, and binding

6 yards of backing fabric

84×106" of quilt batting

Finished quilt top: 77½×100⅛"
Finished block: 12" square

Quantities specified for 44/45"-wide, 100% cotton
fabrics. All measurements include a ¼" seam
allowance. Sew with right sides together unless
otherwise stated.

Cut the Fabrics

To make the best use of your fabrics, cut the pieces
in the order that follows. The patterns are on *Pattern
Sheet 2*. To make templates of the patterns, follow
the instructions in Quilter's Schoolhouse, which
begins on *page 150*.

From *each* assorted red and green print, cut:
- 1—4½" square
- 16—2½" squares

From cream print, cut:
- 72—4½" squares
- 72—2½×4½" rectangles

From dark red print, cut:
- 72—2½×4½" rectangles
- 72—2½" squares

From solid red, cut:
- 16—1½×42" strips for sashing
- 30 of Pattern A
- 9 of Pattern B

continued

From solid green, cut:
- 24—1½×42" strips for sashing and inner border
- 18 of Pattern A
- 8 of Pattern B

From red floral, cut:
- 9—5×42" strips for outer border
- 25—2½×42" strips for sashing and binding
- 3—18¼" squares, cutting each diagonally twice in an X for a total of 12 setting triangles (you'll have 2 leftover triangles)
- 2—9⅜" squares, cutting each in half diagonally for a total of 4 corner triangles
- 24—3¼" squares, cutting each diagonally twice in an X for a total of 96 sashing triangles

Assemble the Blocks

The following instructions result in one block. Repeat the steps to make a total of 18 blocks.

For each block, designer Ann Lage used the same cream print and dark red print. She selected sixteen 2½" squares from one red or green print for the star points in each block, and chose a 4½" square in the same color but a different print for the center.

1. For accurate sewing lines, use a quilter's pencil to mark a diagonal line on the wrong side of sixteen 2½" squares from the same red or green print and four dark red print 2½" squares. (To prevent your fabric from stretching as you draw the lines, place 220-grit sandpaper under the squares.)

2. Align a marked red or green print 2½" square with one end of a cream print 2½×4½" rectangle (see Diagram 1; note the placement of the marked diagonal line). Stitch on the marked line; trim away the excess fabric, leaving a ¼" seam allowance. Press the attached triangle open.

Diagram 1

3. Align a matching marked red or green print 2½" square with the opposite end of the cream print rectangle (see Diagram 1, again noting the placement of the marked diagonal line). Stitch on the marked line; trim and press as before to make a Flying Geese unit A. The pieced Flying Geese unit A should still measure 2½×4½", including the seam allowances.

4. Repeat steps 2 and 3 to make a total of four of Flying Geese unit A.

5. Repeat steps 2 and 3 using the remaining marked red or green print 2½" squares and four dark red print 2½×4½" rectangles to make four of Flying Geese unit B.

6. Referring to Diagram 2 for placement, sew together one Flying Geese unit A and one Flying Geese unit B to make a star point unit. Press the seam allowance in one direction. The pieced star point unit should measure 4½" square, including the seam allowances. Repeat to make a total of four star point units.

Diagram 2

7. Align a marked dark red print 2½" square with one corner of a cream print 4½" square (see Diagram 3; note the placement of the marked diagonal line). Stitch on the marked line; trim away the excess fabric, leaving a ¼" seam allowance. Press the attached triangle open to make a corner unit. The pieced corner unit should still measure 4½" square, including the seam allowances. Repeat to make a total of four corner units.

Diagram 3

8. Referring to Diagram 4, lay out the four star point units, the four corner units, and one assorted red or green print 4½" square in three horizontal rows. Sew together the units in each row. Press the seam allowances toward the center square or corner units. Then join the rows to make a star block. Press the seam allowances in one direction. The pieced star block should measure 12½" square, including the seam allowances.

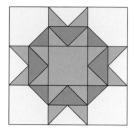

Diagram 4

Assemble the Sashing Units

1. Referring to Diagram 5, sew red floral sashing triangles to opposite edges of a solid green A piece to make a triangle unit. Press the seam allowances toward the A piece. Repeat to make a second triangle unit. Then join the triangle units to the long edges of a solid red B piece to make a Sashing Unit A. Pieced Sashing Unit A should measure 4½" square, including seam allowances. Repeat to make a total of nine of Sashing Unit A.

Diagram 5
Sashing Unit A

2. Referring to Diagram 6, sew red floral sashing triangles to opposite edges of a solid red A piece to make a triangle unit. Press the seam allowances toward the A piece. Repeat to make a second triangle unit. Then join the triangle units to the long edges of a solid green B piece to make a Sashing Unit B. Repeat to make a total of eight of Sashing Unit B.

Diagram 6
Sashing Unit B

3. Referring to Diagram 7, sew red floral sashing triangles to opposite edges of a solid red A piece to make a Sashing Unit C. Press the seam allowances toward the A piece. Repeat to make a total of 14 of Sashing Unit C.

Diagram 7
Sashing Unit C

Assemble the Sashing Strips

1. Referring to Diagram 8, sew together a solid green 1½×42" strip, a red floral 2½×42" strip, and a solid red 1½×42" strip to make a strip set. Press the seam allowances in one direction. Repeat to make a total of 16 strip sets.

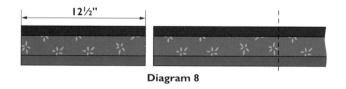

Diagram 8

2. Cut the strip sets into 12½"-wide segments to make a total of 48 pieced 4½×12½" sashing strips.

Assemble the Quilt Center

1. Referring to the photograph *above* for placement, lay out the 18 blocks, the 31 pieced sashing units,

continued

the 48 pieced sashing strips, and 10 red floral setting triangles in diagonal rows.

2. Sew together the pieces in each row. Press the seam allowances toward the sashing strips.

3. Join the rows. Press the seam allowances toward the sashing rows. Add the four red floral corner triangles to complete the quilt center. The pieced quilt center should measure 67×89⅝", including the seam allowances.

Add the Borders

1. Cut and piece the remaining solid green 1½×42" strips to make the following:
   - 2—1½×89⅝" inner border strips
   - 2—1½×69" inner border strips

2. Sew the long inner border strips to the side edges of the pieced quilt center. Then add the short inner border strips to the top and bottom edges of the pieced quilt center. Press the seam allowances toward the solid green inner border.

3. Cut and piece the red floral 5×42" strips to make the following:
   - 2—5×91⅝" outer border strips
   - 2—5×78" outer border strips

4. Sew the long outer border strips to the side edges of the pieced quilt center. Then add the short outer border strips to the top and bottom edges of the pieced quilt center to complete the quilt top. Press the seam allowances toward the floral outer border.

Complete the Quilt

1. Layer the quilt top, batting, and backing according to the instructions in Quilter's Schoolhouse, which begins on *page 150*. Quilt as desired.

2. Use the remaining red floral 2½×42" strips to bind the quilt according to the instructions in Quilter's Schoolhouse.

Abby's Wish Quilt
optional sizes

If you'd like to make this quilt in a size other than for a double bed, use the information *below*.

Alternate quilt sizes	Wall	Throw	Queen/King
Number of blocks	5	13	25
Number of blocks wide by long	2×2	3×3	4×4
Finished size	54⅞" square	77½" square	100⅛" square
Yardage requirements			
Number of 9×22" pieces of assorted red and green prints	5	13	25
Cream print	¾ yard	1½ yards	2⅝ yards
Dark red print	½ yard	1 yard	1⅝ yards
Solid red	⅝ yard	1 yard	1½ yards
Solid green	⅞ yard	1¼ yards	1¾ yards
Red floral	2⅞ yards	3¾ yards	5½ yards
Backing	3½ yards	4⅔ yards	9 yards
Batting	61" square	84" square	107" square

PASTEL THROW

Reproduction 1930s fabrics compose each "Abby's Wish" star.

Materials

1⅓ yards of solid white for blocks

12—⅛-yard pieces of assorted pink, blue, red, green, peach, purple, and aqua solids for blocks

12—¼-yard pieces of assorted pink, blue, red, green, peach, purple, and aqua prints for blocks and outer border

1⅛ yards of solid yellow for inner border, sashing, and binding

3¼ yards of backing fabric

58×72" of quilt batting

Finished quilt top: 52½×66"

continued

From solid yellow, cut:
- 6—2½×42" binding strips
- 3—1¾×42" strips for inner border
- 2—2×38½" inner border strips
- 3—1½×38½" sashing strips
- 8—1½×12½" sashing strips

Assemble the Blocks

1. Referring to Assemble the Blocks on *page 98*, steps 1 through 3, use eight assorted solid 2½" squares and four solid white 2½×4½" rectangles to make a total of four of Flying Geese unit A. Use eight assorted solid 2½" squares and four assorted print 2½×4½" rectangles to make a total of four of Flying Geese unit B. *Note:* To make one star block, you will pair one solid with one print.

2. Referring to Diagram 2 on *page 98,* sew together one Flying Geese unit A and one Flying Geese unit B to make a star point unit. Repeat to make a total of four star point units.

3. Referring to Step 7 on *page 98,* use four assorted print 2½" squares and four solid white 4½" squares to make a total of four corner units.

4. Referring to Diagram 4 on *page 99,* lay out the four star point units, the four corner units, and one assorted print 4½" square in three rows. Sew together the units in each row. Then join the rows to make a star block. The pieced star block should measure 12½" square, including the seam allowances.

5. Repeat steps 1 to 4 to make a total of 12 star blocks.

Assemble the Quilt Center

1. Lay out the 12 pieced blocks and the eight solid yellow 1½×12½" sashing strips in four horizontal rows.

2. Sew together the pieces in each row. Press the seam allowances toward the sashing strips.

3. Join the rows with the three solid yellow 1½×38½" sashing strips to make the quilt center. Press the seam allowances toward the sashing strips. The pieced quilt center should measure 38½×51½", including the seam allowances.

Cut the Fabrics

To make the best use of your fabrics, cut the pieces in the order that follows.

From solid white, cut:
- 48—4½" squares
- 48—2½×4½" rectangles

From *each* assorted solid, cut:
- 16—2½" squares

From *each* assorted print, cut:
- 1—4½" square
- 12—2×6½" rectangles (you'll have 2 leftover rectangles)
- 4—2½×4½" rectangles
- 4—2½" squares

Add the Borders

1. Sew the solid yellow 2×38½" inner border strips to the top and bottom edges of the quilt center.

2. Cut and piece the solid yellow 1¾×42" strips to make the following:
   - 2—1¾×54½" inner border strips

3. Sew the solid yellow inner border strips to the side edges of the quilt center. Press all the seam allowances toward the inner border.

4. Sew together 27 assorted print 2×6½" rectangles to make a 6½×41" border strip. Repeat to make a second border strip. Join the border strips to the top and bottom edges of the quilt center.

5. Sew together 44 assorted print 2×6½" rectangles to make a 6½×66½" side border strip. Repeat to make a second side border strip. Join the side border strips to the quilt center.

Complete the Quilt

1. Layer the quilt top, batting, and backing according to the instructions in Quilter's Schoolhouse, which begins on *page 150*. Quilt as desired.

2. Use the solid yellow 2½×42" strips to bind the quilt according to the instructions in Quilter's Schoolhouse.

STAR PILLOWS

An "Abby's Wish" star radiates from each

of these red, white, and blue throw pillows.

Materials for Dark Blue Pillow

Scrap of blue large floral for block

9×22" piece (fat eighth) of red check for block

9×22" piece (fat eighth) of blue check for block

9×22" piece (fat eighth) of blue small floral for block

9×22" piece (fat eighth) of blue print for block

½ yard of dark blue print for border and

    pillow back

⅜ yard of solid red for covered cording

18" square of muslin for lining

18" square of quilt batting

2 yards of ½"-diameter cording

16" square pillow form

Finished pillow: 16" square

continued

Cut the Fabrics

To make the best use of your fabrics, cut the pieces in the order that follows.

From blue large floral, cut:
- 1—4½" square

From red check, cut:
- 8—2½" squares

From blue check, cut:
- 8—2½" squares

From blue small floral, cut:
- 4—2½×4½" rectangles
- 4—2½" squares

From blue print, cut:
- 4—4½" squares
- 4—2½×4½" rectangles

From dark blue print, cut:
- 1—16½" square for pillow back
- 2—2½×16½" border strips
- 2—2½×12½" border strips

From solid red, cut:
- 1—13" square, cutting and piecing it into enough 1½"-wide bias strips to total 72" in length (For specific instructions see Cutting Bias Strips in Quilter's Schoolhouse, which begins on *page 150*.)

Assemble the Block

1. Referring to Assemble the Blocks on *page 98*, steps 1 through 3, use eight red check 2½" squares and four blue small floral 2½×4½" rectangles to make a total of four of Flying Geese unit A. Use the eight blue check 2½" squares and four blue print 2½×4½" rectangles to make a total of four of Flying Geese unit B.

2. Referring to Diagram 2 on *page 98*, sew together one Flying Geese unit A and one Flying Geese unit B to make a star point unit. Repeat to make a total of four star point units.

3. Referring to Step 7 on *page 98*, use four blue small floral 2½" squares and four blue print 4½" squares to make a total of four corner units.

4. Referring to Diagram 4 on *page 99*, lay out the four star point units, the four corner units, and the blue large floral 4½" square in three rows. Sew together the units in each row. Press the seam allowances toward the center square or corner units. Then join the rows to make a star block. Press the seam allowances in one direction. The pieced star block should measure 12½" square, including the seam allowances.

Add the Border

Sew the dark blue print 2½×12½" border strips to opposite edges of the star block. Then join the dark blue print 2½×16½" border strips to the remaining edges of the block to complete the pillow top. Press all the seam allowances toward the border.

Complete the Pillow

1. Layer the pillow top, batting, and 18" square muslin lining according to the directions in Quilter's Schoolhouse, which begins on *page 150*. Quilt as desired. Trim the excess batting and muslin even with the edges of the pillow top.

2. Cover the cording with the pieced solid red 1½×72" bias strip to create 72" of covered cording (see Quilter's Schoolhouse for instructions).

3. Aligning raw edges and using a machine cording foot, stitch the covered cording to the pillow top.

4. Sew together the pillow top and the dark blue print 16½" square pillow back, leaving an opening to insert the pillow form. Turn right side out and insert the pillow form through the opening. Whipstitch the opening closed.

Materials for Light Blue Pillow

Scrap of blue large floral for block

⅜ yard of dark blue print for block and
    covered cording

9×22" piece (fat eighth) of red check for block

9×22" piece (fat eighth) of blue small floral for block

½ yard of blue stripe for border and pillow back

18" square of muslin for lining

18" square of quilt batting

2 yards of ½"-diameter cording

16" square pillow form

Finished pillow: 16" square

Cut the Fabrics

To make the best use of your fabrics, cut the pieces
in the order that follows.

From blue large floral, cut:
- 4½" square

From dark blue print, cut:
- 1   13" square, cutting and piecing it into
  enough 1½"-wide bias strips to total 72" in length
  (For specific instructions see Cutting Bias Strips
  in Quilter's Schoolhouse, which begins on
  page 150.)
- 16—2½" squares

From red check, cut:
- 4—2½×4½" rectangles
- 4—2½" squares

From blue small floral, cut:
- 4—4½" squares
- 4—2½×4½" rectangles

From blue stripe, cut:
- 1—16½" square for pillow back
- 2—2½×16½" border strips
- 2—2½×12½" border strips

Assemble the Block

1. Referring to Assemble the Blocks on *page 98,*
   steps 1 through 3, use eight dark blue print 2½"
   squares and four red check 2½×4½" rectangles to
   make a total of four of Flying Geese unit A. Use
   eight dark blue print 2½" squares and four blue
   small floral 2½×4½" rectangles to make a total of
   four of Flying Geese unit B.

2. Referring to Diagram 2 on *page 98,* sew together
   one Flying Geese unit A and one Flying Geese
   unit B to make a star point unit. Repeat to make
   a total of four star point units.

3. Referring to Step 7 on *page 98,* use four red
   check 2½" squares and four blue small floral
   4½" squares to make a total of four corner units.

4. Referring to Diagram 4 on *page 99,* lay out the
   four star point units, four corner units, and blue
   large floral 4½" square. Join the units in each row.
   Press the seam allowances toward the center
   square or corner units. Then join the rows to
   make a star block. Press the seam allowances
   in one direction. The pieced star block
   should measure 12½" square, including the
   seam allowances.

Add the Border

Sew the blue stripe 2½×12½" border strips to
opposite edges of the star block. Then join the blue
stripe 2½×16½" border strips to the remaining edges
of the block to complete the pillow top. Press all the
seam allowances toward the border.

Complete the Pillow

Referring to Complete the Pillow *opposite,* use the
dark blue print pieced 1½×72" bias strip to make the
covered cording and finish the pillow.

Brilliant Trip Around the World

Carla Malkiewicz designed this brightly colored project for an Amish quilt challenge held by a quilt shop. Carla combined her specialty, bargello—a patchwork design that results in a zigzag or flame pattern— with the traditional Trip Around the World pattern.

Materials

1—2½" square of solid burgundy (A) for center

⅓ yard *each* of solid light pink (B), pink (C), dark pink (D), red (E), orange (F), yellow (G), blue (H), light blue (I), blue-green (J), dark green (K), green (L), yellow-green (M), and navy (N) for rows and middle border

3⅝ yards of solid black for sashing strips, inner border, outer border, and binding

3¾ yards of backing fabric

67×79" of quilt batting

Finished quilt top: 60½×72½"

Quantities specified for 44/45"-wide, 100% cotton fabrics. All measurements include a ¼" seam allowance. Sew with right sides together unless otherwise stated.

Cut the Fabrics

To make the best use of your fabrics, cut the pieces in the order that follows on *page 108*. There are no pattern pieces for this project; the letter designations are for placement purposes only.

Cut the sashing and border strips the length of the fabric (parallel to the selvage).

continued

From solid light pink (B), cut:
- 48—2½" squares
- 10—1¼×2½" rectangles

From solid pink (C), cut:
- 48—2½" squares
- 10—1¼×2½" rectangles

From solid dark pink (D), cut:
- 48—2½" squares
- 10—1¼×2½" rectangles

From solid red (E), cut:
- 48—2½" squares
- 10—1¼×2½" rectangles

From solid orange (F), cut:
- 48—2½" squares
- 10—1¼×2½" rectangles

From solid yellow (G), cut:
- 48—2½" squares
- 10—1¼×2½" rectangles

From solid blue (H), cut:
- 48—2½" squares
- 10—1¼×2½" rectangles

From solid light blue (I), cut:
- 48—2½" squares
- 10—1¼×2½" rectangles

From solid blue-green (J), cut:
- 48—2½" squares
- 10—1¼×2½" rectangles

From solid dark green (K), cut:
- 48—2½" squares
- 10—1¼×2½" rectangles

From solid green (L), cut:
- 48—2½" squares
- 10—1¼×2½" rectangles

From solid yellow-green (M), cut:
- 48—2½" squares
- 10—1¼×2½" rectangles

From solid navy (N), cut:
- 48—2½" squares
- 10—1¼×2½" rectangles

From solid black, cut:
- 7—2½×42" binding strips
- 2—4×73" outer border strips
- 2—4×54" outer border strips
- 2—1½×64½" inner border strips
- 2—1½×50½" inner border strips
- 24—1×50½" sashing strips

Assemble the Quilt Center

1. Referring to the Quilt Assembly Diagram *opposite* for placement, lay out all of the 2½" squares in 25 horizontal rows according to the alphabetical designations.

2. Sew together the squares in each row. Press the seam allowances in one direction.

3. Join the rows to make the quilt center, alternating pieced rows with black 1×50½" sashing strips. Press all seam allowances toward the black sashing strips. The pieced quilt center should measure 50½×62½", including the seam allowances.

Add the Borders

1. Sew the black 1½×50½" inner border strips to the top and bottom edges of the pieced quilt center. Then add the black 1½×64½" inner border strips to the side edges of the pieced quilt center. Press all seam allowances toward the black inner border.

2. Piece the assorted solid color 1¼×2½" rectangles, maintaining the same color progression as in the quilt top, to make the following:
- 2—1¼×52½" middle border strips
- 2—1¼×66" middle border strips

3. Sew the short pieced middle border strips to the top and bottom edges of the pieced quilt center. Then add the long pieced middle border strips to the side edges of the pieced quilt center. Press all seam allowances toward the black inner border.

4. Sew the black 4×54" outer border strips to the top and bottom edges of the pieced quilt center. Then add the black 4×73" outer border strips to the side edges of the pieced quilt center to complete the quilt top. Press all seam allowances toward the black outer border.

Complete the Quilt

1. Layer the quilt top, batting, and backing according to the instructions in Quilter's Schoolhouse, which begins on *page 150*.

2. Quilt as desired. Designer Carla Malkiewicz machine-quilted this project in an allover feather design using variegated thread.

3. Use the solid black 2½×42" strips to bind the quilt according to the instructions in Quilter's Schoolhouse.

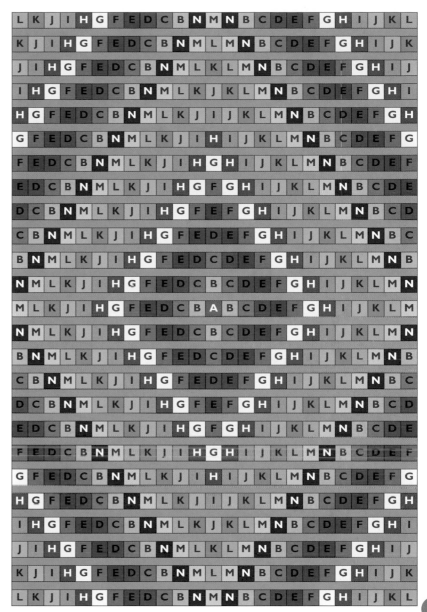

Quilt Assembly Diagram

optional colors

Quilt tester Laura Boehnke created her version of this project for the quiltmaker who prefers a softer palette of springlike colors.

"I could see this in a bed size for a child; you could use fun prints and vibrant colors," Laura says. "Or you could do a color wash; it would be interesting to see what the lines separating everything would do to it."

The narrow sashing strips intrigue Laura. "They give you a visual gap between the rows so if you're off a smidge, it's OK," she says.

ART TRIO

Splashes of gray, black, and red stairstep their way across

this contemporary three-panel wall hanging.

Materials

1—2½" square of black print (fabric A)

2—¼-yard pieces of black prints (F, N) for rows

6—¼-yard pieces of gray prints (B, C, D, E, L, M) for rows

5—¼-yard pieces of red prints (G, H, I, J, K) for rows

⅞ yard of solid black for sashing strips and borders

1¾ yards of backing fabric

3—21×41" pieces of quilt batting

Finished wall hanging: 45×35"
Finished quilt panel: 15×35"

Cut the Fabrics

To make the best use of your fabrics, cut the pieces in the order that follows. There are no pattern pieces for this project; the letter designations are for placement only. A specific fabric is used for each lettered square.

From black prints, cut:
- 19—2½" squares (F)
- 17—2½" squares (N)

From gray prints, cut:
- 18—2½" squares (B)
- 19—2½" squares (C)
- 20—2½" squares (D)
- 20—2½" squares (E)
- 18—2½" squares (L)
- 18—2½" squares (M)

From red prints, cut:
- 18—2½" squares (G)
- 18—2½" squares (H)
- 18—2½" squares (I)
- 18—2½" squares (J)
- 18—2½" squares (K)

From solid black, cut:
- 8—2×42" strips for borders
- 12—1×32½" sashing strips

Assemble the Quilt Center Panels

1. Referring to the Quilt Assembly Diagram for placement, lay out all of the 2½" squares in five vertical rows for each of the three panels according to the letter designations.

2. Sew together the pieces in each row. Press the seam allowances in one direction. Join the rows and four solid black 1×32½" sashing strips for each panel to make three quilt centers. Press the seam allowances toward the solid black sashing strips. Each pieced quilt center should measure 12½×32½", including the seam allowances.

  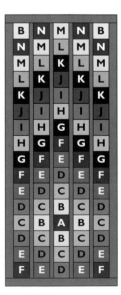

Quilt Assembly Diagram

Add the Borders

1. Cut the solid black 2×42" strips to make the following:
   - 6—2×35½" border strips
   - 6—2×12½" border strips

2. Sew the short solid black border strips to the top and bottom edges of each pieced quilt center. Then add the long solid black border strips to the side edges of each pieced quilt center. Press all the seam allowances toward the borders.

Complete Each Panel

1. Layer each panel and backing, right sides together, with batting on top. Sew together the layers, leaving a 5" opening. Turn the panels right sides out; press. Slip-stitch the openings closed. Topstitch ⅜" from all edges. Quilt as desired.

2. Add a hanging sleeve to the back of each panel to complete the panels. For specific instructions on making a hanging sleeve, see Quilter's Schoolhouse, which begins on *page 150*.

VALANCE

Liven up a room with this window valance inspired by the "Brilliant Trip Around the World" pattern.

Materials

6—¼-yard pieces of purple prints (A, B, C, E, K, L) for rows

2—¼-yard pieces of tan prints (D, I) for rows

2—¼-yard pieces of brown prints (G, J) for rows

3—¼-yard pieces of green prints (H, M, N) for rows

3¾ yards of dark green print (F) for rows, sashing strips, border, and lining

Finished valance: 22×112½"

Cut the Fabrics

To make the best use of your fabrics, cut the pieces in the order that follows. There are no pattern pieces for this project; the letter designations are for placement only. A specific fabric is used for each lettered square.

Cut the dark green print sashing and border strips and lining the length of the fabric (parallel to the selvage).

From purple print (A), cut:
- 20—2½" squares
- 4—1¼×2½" rectangles

From purple print (B), cut:
- 20—2½" squares
- 4—1¼×2½" rectangles

From purple print (C), cut:
- 20—2½" squares
- 4—1¼×2½" rectangles

From purple print (E), cut:
- 25—2½" squares
- 2—1¼×2½" rectangles

From purple print (K), cut:
- 19—2½" squares
- 8—1¼×2½" rectangles

From purple print (L), cut:
- 19—2½" squares
- 8—1¼×2½" rectangles

From tan print (D), cut:
- 20—2½" squares
- 2—1¼×2½" rectangles

From tan print (I), cut:
- 12—2½" squares
- 8—1¼×2½" rectangles

From brown print (G), cut:
- 20—2½" squares
- 2—1¼×2½" rectangles

From brown print (J), cut:
- 18—2½" squares
- 6—1¼×2½" rectangles

From green print (H), cut:
- 16—2½" squares
- 4—1¼×2½" rectangles

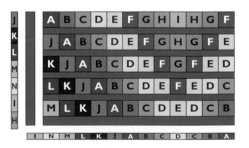

From green print (M), cut:
- 13—2½" squares
- 6—1¼×2½" rectangles

From green print (N), cut:
- 10—2½" squares
- 7—1¼×2½" rectangles

From dark green print (F), cut:
- 1—22½×113" rectangle for lining
- 1—5½×113" top border strip
- 1—3½×113" bottom border strip
- 4—1×102½" sashing strips
- 1—1¾×102½" sashing strip
- 2—3×14½" side border strips
- 2—2½×13¾" sashing strips
- 23—2½" squares
- 2—1¼×2½" rectangles

Assemble the Valance Front

1. Referring to the Valance Center Assembly Diagram for placement, lay out all of the 2½" squares in five horizontal rows according to the letter designations.

2. Sew together the squares in each row. Press the seam allowances in one direction. Join the pieced rows and the four dark green print 1×102½" sashing strips; add the dark green print 1¾×102½" sashing strip to the bottom edge to make the valance center. Press the seam allowances in one direction.

3. Sew the dark green print 2½×13¾" sashing strips to the side edges of the valance center. The pieced valance center should measure 13¾×106½", including the seam allowances.

4. Referring to the Valance Center Assembly Diagram, lay out the fifty-three 1¼×2½" rectangles in a horizontal row according to the letter designations; join. Press the seam allowances in one direction. Sew the pieced row to the bottom edge of the valance center.

5. Lay out fourteen 1¼×2½" rectangles in two vertical rows according to the letter designations in the Valance Center Assembly Diagram. Press the seam allowances in one direction. Sew the pieced rows to the side edges of the valance center.

6. Sew the dark green print 3×14½" border strips to the side edges of the valance center. Sew the dark green print 5½×113" border strip to the top edge of the valance center and the dark green print 3½×113" border strip to the bottom edge of the valance center to complete the valance front. Press the seam allowances toward the dark green border.

Complete the Valance

1. With right sides together, sew together the pieced valance front and the dark green print 22½×113" lining rectangle, leaving a 5" opening at the top on both side edges for turning and the rod casing. Turn the valance right side out; press.

2. Referring to the Valance Rod Pocket Diagram, turn the openings' raw edges to the inside; stitch each edge separately to finish the edges of the rod casing. Topstitch along the top edge of the pieced center panel to make the lower edge of the rod casing. Topstitch 3" up from the first row of topstitching to make the top edge of the rod casing. Slip-stitch the openings closed above the rod casing to complete the valance.

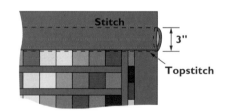

Valance Rod Pocket Diagram

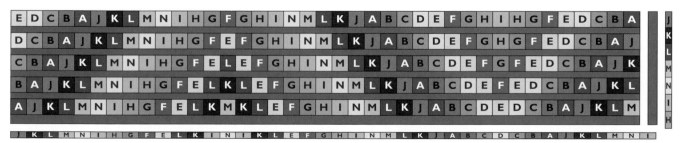

Valance Center Assembly Diagram

HEAVEN'S *Stairway*

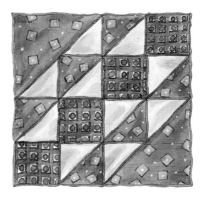

Triangles and squares dance across this fanciful quilt created by designer

Jill Reber. She used bright prints and coordinating fabrics from her stash and

lightened the look with solid white.

Materials

48—18×22" pieces (fat quarters) of assorted

   bright prints for blocks and borders

4¼ yards of solid white for blocks, borders,

   and binding

5 yards of backing fabric

74×90" of quilt batting

Finished quilt top: 68×84"
Finished block: 8" square

Quantities specified for 44/45"-wide, 100% cotton fabrics. All measurements include a ¼" seam allowance. Sew with right sides together unless otherwise stated.

Designer Tips

Quiltmaker Jill Reber pieced this scrappy quilt in a controlled manner. Before cutting the bright prints, she sorted them into 24 sets of two complementary colors. Once the sets were cut, she created two blocks from each set, reversing the prints' placement in each.

Cut the Fabrics

To make the best use of your fabrics, cut the pieces in the order that follows.

From *each* assorted bright print, cut:
- 1—4⅞" square, cutting it in half diagonally for a total of 2 large triangles
- 3—2⅞" squares, cutting each in half diagonally for a total of 6 small triangles
- 7—2½" squares (you'll have 12 leftover)

From solid white, cut:
- 8—4½×42" strips for outer border
- 14—2½×42" strips for inner border and binding
- 240—2⅞" squares, cutting each in half diagonally for a total of 480 small triangles
- 128—2½" squares

continued

Assemble the Blocks

Pair your assorted bright print pieces into 24 sets of two fabrics each.

The following instructions combine solid white pieces and the pieces in one fabric set (a purple print and yellow print, in this case) into two blocks. Repeat these steps for each of your 24 fabric sets to make a total of 48 blocks.

1. Join one purple print small triangle and one solid white small triangle to make a purple-and-white triangle-square (see Diagram 1). Press the seam allowance toward the purple print. Repeat to make a total of six purple-and-white triangle-squares.

Diagram 1

2. Referring to Diagram 2 for placement, sew together two yellow print 2½" squares and two purple-and-white triangle-squares in pairs. Press the seam allowances toward the yellow print squares. Then join the pairs to make a unit 1. Press the seam allowance in one direction. Repeat to make a second unit 1.

Diagram 2

3. Referring to Diagram 3, sew together two solid white small triangles and a purple-and-white triangle-square to make a pieced large triangle. Press the seam allowances in one direction.

Diagram 3

4. Sew a purple print large triangle to the pieced large triangle to make a unit 2. Press the seam allowance toward the purple print triangle. Repeat to make a second unit 2.

5. Referring to Diagram 4, lay out two of unit 1 and two of unit 2 in pairs; sew together. Press the seam allowances toward unit 2. Then join the

pairs to make a block. Press the seam allowance in one direction. The pieced block should measure 8½" square, including seam allowances.

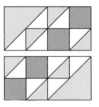

Diagram 4

6. Referring to Diagram 5, repeat steps 1 through 5, reversing the placement of the yellow and purple prints, to make a second block.

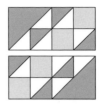

Diagram 5

Assemble the Quilt Center

1. Referring to the photograph *opposite* for placement, lay out the 48 pieced blocks in eight horizontal rows.

2. Sew together the blocks in each row. Press the seam allowances in each row in one direction, alternating the direction with each row.

3. Join the rows to make the quilt center. Press the seam allowances in one direction. The pieced quilt center should measure 48½x64½", including the seam allowances.

Assemble and Add the Borders

1. Cut and piece six solid white 2½x42" strips to make the following.
- 2—2½x64½" inner border strips
- 2—2½x48½" inner border strips

2. Sew the short inner border strips to the top and bottom edges of the pieced quilt center.

3. Sew a bright print 2½" square to each end of the long inner border strips to make two pieced inner border strips.

Heaven's Stairway

4. Add the pieced inner border strips to the side edges of the pieced quilt center. Press the seam allowances toward the solid white inner border.

5. Referring to Diagram 6, pair a solid white 2½" square and a bright print 2½" square; sew together. Press the seam allowance toward the bright print square. Repeat to make a second pair. Join the pairs to make a Four-Patch block. The pieced Four-Patch block should measure 4½" square, including the seam allowances.

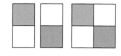

Diagram 6

6. Repeat Step 5 to make a total of 64 Four-Patch blocks.

7. Referring to the photograph *right*, join 13 Four-Patch blocks to make a top middle border strip that measures 4½×52½", including the seam allowances. Repeat to make a bottom middle border strip. Sew the pieced middle border strips to the top and bottom edges of the pieced quilt center. Press the seam allowances toward the solid white inner border.

8. Join 19 Four-Patch blocks to make a side middle border strip that measures 4½×76½", including the seam allowances. Repeat to make a second side middle border strip. Sew the pieced side middle border strips to the side edges of the pieced quilt center. Press the seam allowances toward the solid white inner border.

9. Cut and piece the solid white 4½×42" strips to make the following:
- 2—4½×84½" outer border strips
- 2—4½×60½" outer border strips

10. Sew the short outer border strips to the top and bottom edges of the pieced quilt center. Then sew the long outer border strips to the side edges of the pieced quilt center to complete the quilt top. Press all seam allowances toward the solid white outer border.

Complete the Quilt

1. Layer the quilt top, batting, and backing according to the instructions in Quilter's Schoolhouse, which begins on *page 150*.

2. Quilt as desired. The center and middle border of Jill's project was machine-quilted with a meandering stitch. A leaf-and-vine pattern was quilted on the solid white inner border, and a flower pattern was quilted on the solid white outer border.

3. Use the remaining solid white 2½×42" strips to bind the quilt according to the instructions in Quilter's Schoolhouse.

continued

Heaven's Stairway Quilt
optional sizes

If you'd like to make this quilt in a size other than for a twin bed, use the information *below*.

Alternate quilt sizes	Crib/Lap	Full/Queen	King
Number of blocks	15	81	100
Number of blocks wide by long	3×5	9×9	10×10
Finished size	44×60"	92" square	100" square
Yardage requirements			
Number of 18×22" pieces of assorted bright prints	16	82	100
Solid white	2½ yards	5¾ yards	6⅔ yards
Backing	2⅞ yards	8¼ yards	8⅞ yards
Batting	50×66"	98" square	106" square

BED QUILT

Brightly colored prints and controlled placement of the block from "Heaven's Stairway" create dynamic movement across this quilt.

Materials

3 yards of purple print for blocks

3⅜ yards total of assorted yellow-and-green prints for blocks

1¾ yards total of assorted rose prints for blocks

⅔ yard of yellow print for binding

5¼ yards of backing fabric

70×94" of quilt batting

Finished quilt top: 64×88"

Cut the Fabrics

To make the best use of your fabrics, cut the pieces in the order that follows.

From purple print, cut:

• 440—2⅞" squares, cutting each in half diagonally for a total of 880 small triangles

From assorted yellow-and-green prints, cut:

• 88—4⅞" squares, cutting each in half diagonally for a total of 176 large triangles

• 264—2⅞" squares, cutting each in half diagonally for a total of 528 small triangles

From assorted rose prints, cut:

• 352—2½" squares

From yellow print, cut:

• 8—2½×42" binding strips

Assemble the Blocks

1. Referring to Assemble the Blocks on *page 116*, Step 1, use one purple print small triangle and one yellow-and-green print small triangle to make a triangle-square. Repeat to make a total of six triangle-squares.

2. Referring to Diagram 2 on *page 116*, sew together two rose print 2½" squares and two triangle-squares in pairs. Then join the pairs to make a unit 1. Repeat to make a second unit 1.

3. Referring to Diagram 3 on *page 116*, sew together two purple print small triangles and a triangle-square to make a pieced large triangle. Sew a yellow-and-green print large triangle to the pieced large triangle to make a unit 2. Repeat to make a second unit 2.

4. Lay out two of unit 1 and two of unit 2 in pairs (see Diagram 4 on *page 116*); sew together. Then join the pairs to make a block.

5. Repeat steps 1 through 4 to make a total of 88 blocks.

Assemble the Quilt Top

1. Referring to the photograph *opposite* for placement, lay out the 88 pieced blocks in 11 horizontal rows.

2. Sew together the blocks in each row. Press the seam allowances in one direction, alternating the direction with each row.

3. Join the rows to make the quilt top. Press the seam allowances in one direction. The pieced quilt top should measure 64½×88½", including the seam allowances.

Complete the Quilt

1. Layer the quilt top, batting, and backing according to the instructions in Quilter's Schoolhouse. Quilt as desired.

2. Use the yellow print 2½×42" strips to bind the quilt according to the instructions in Quilter's Schoolhouse.

MAKE IT YOUR WAY

Play with the placement of your quilt blocks and choose the colors of your fabrics

carefully for a beautiful quilt that is uniquely yours.

Y ou can create dynamic quilt designs simply by rotating a single block or by changing the color of the fabrics used in each block. Each of the six eye-catching quilt designs shown *below* and *opposite* involve a different placement of the "Heaven's Stairway" block, *above*. The chosen fabric colors further enhance each overall pattern.

Block Placement Magic
Rotating a block reveals its versatility. In these quilt designs, zigzags, Xs, diamond shapes, strong diagonal lines of color, and patterns on point

emerge when the same block is placed in different positions. Repeating positions or creating mirror images of the block deliver surprising and pleasing arrangements.

Choose Colors Carefully
The design possibilities expand when more colors are added or when color placement varies. It is important to choose colors that appeal to you and suit the design. For example, a block design may create a distinct pattern with unusual colors, but may not be as visually pleasing.

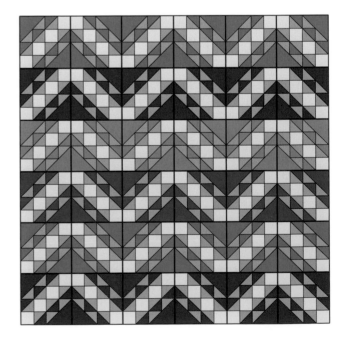

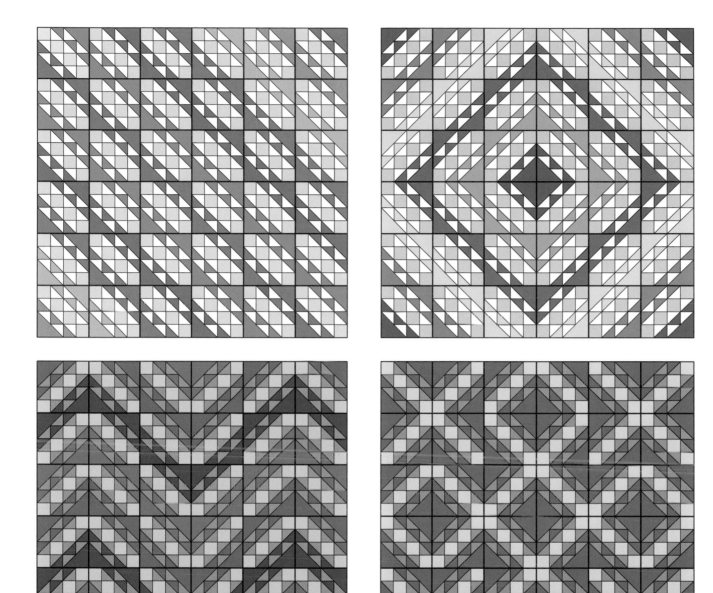

Check for Contrast

Although color is fun, it is contrast, or differences
in values, that often makes a design successful.
Without contrast in value between pieces in a block
or the blocks in a quilt top, the colors will blend
together and the design itself may get lost. Learn
to see fabrics in light, medium, and dark values so
when you select fabrics for a quilt, you end up
with a more satisfying quilt design.

Take a Step Back

One of the best ways to tell if your fabric or color
combination will work in a quilt is to place the
blocks on a design wall and step back from them to
visualize how they will look—and work—together.
Fabrics that don't appear to work when viewed up
close may be perfect from a distance, where you can
see each fabric's contribution to the whole.

ANYTIME APPLIQUÉ

Play around with appliqué, and you'll soon discover a multitude of methods, whether you prefer stitching by hand or by machine. "Tiger Lily," "Serendipity," and "Sweet Lullabies" offer numerous possibilities for using fusible web, accenting felted wool with embroidery stitches, and combining piecing and appliquéing techniques.

TIGER *Lily*

Inspired by an antique quilt in a photograph, designer Jan Ragaller created

a modern-day version using fusible appliqué, machine blanket stitching, and the

help of several friends who contributed finished blocks.

Materials

4—⅓-yard pieces of rust prints for appliqués

4—⅓-yard pieces of blue prints for appliqués

5—⅓-yard pieces of green prints for appliqués

6½ yards of tan print for appliqué foundations, sashing, and border

2 yards of rust polka dot for blocks, sashing, border, and binding

6⅛ yards of backing fabric

87" square of quilt batting

4 yards of lightweight fusible web

Finished quilt top: 81" square
Finished block: 9¾" square

Quantities specified for 44/45"-wide, 100% cotton fabrics. All measurements include a ¼" seam allowance. Sew with right sides together unless otherwise stated.

Cut the Fabrics

To make the best use of your fabrics, cut the pieces in the order that follows. Cut the sashing and inner border strips the length of the fabric (parallel to the selvage). The patterns are on *Pattern Sheet 2*.

To use fusible web for appliquéing, as was done in this project, complete the following steps.

1. Lay the fusible web, paper side up, over the patterns. Use a pencil to trace each pattern the number of times specified on *page 126*, leaving ½" between tracings. Cut out the pieces roughly ¼" outside the traced lines.

2. Following the manufacturer's instructions, press the fusible-web pieces onto the backs of the designated fabrics; let cool. Cut out the fabric shapes on the drawn lines. Peel off the paper backings.

continued

From rust prints, cut:
- 59 of Pattern A

From blue prints, cut:
- 49 of Pattern A

From green prints, cut:
- 108 of Pattern B
- 72 *each* of patterns C and D
- 36 *each* of patterns E, F, and G

From tan print, cut:
- 2—3½×75½" sashing strips
- 4—3½×69½" sashing strips
- 6—3½×21½" sashing strips
- 36—10¼" squares for appliqué foundations
- 36—2×10¼" sashing strips
- 52—3⅞" squares, cutting each in half diagonally for a total of 104 triangles

From rust polka dot, cut:
- 9—2½×42" binding strips
- 52—3⅞" squares, cutting each in half diagonally for a total of 104 triangles
- 36—3½" squares
- 9—2" squares for sashing

Appliqué the Flower Blocks

1. Referring to the Appliqué Placement Diagram on *Pattern Sheet 2*, lay out the appliqué pieces for one block on a tan print 10¼" square appliqué foundation. Designer Jan Ragaller placed the main stem diagonally on the foundation with the stem's base 1¼" from the corner. The placement of the rust and blue flowers in each block is random, but each block should have at least one of each color. Fuse the appliqués in place.

2. Using threads that match the fabrics, machine-blanket-stitch around each appliqué shape.

3. Fold a rust polka-dot 3½" square in half diagonally. Lightly finger-press to create a stitching guide; unfold. With right

Diagram 1

sides together, align the rust polka-dot square in the corner of the appliquéd square where the main stem ends (see Diagram 1, noting placement of the diagonal line). Stitch on the pressed line; trim the seam allowance to ¼". Press open the remaining triangle to make a flower block. The appliquéd flower block should measure 10¼" square, including the seam allowances.

4. Repeat steps 1 through 3 to make a total of 36 flower blocks.

Assemble the Block Units

1. Referring to Diagram 2 for placement, lay out four flower blocks, four tan print 2×10¼" sashing strips, and one rust polka-dot 2" sashing square in three horizontal rows.

Diagram 2

2. Sew together the pieces in each row. Press the seam allowances in each row in one direction, alternating the direction with each row. Then join the rows to make a block unit. Press the seam allowances in one direction. The pieced block unit should measure 21½" square, including the seam allowances.

3. Repeat steps 1 and 2 to make a total of nine block units.

Assemble the Quilt Center

1. Referring to the Quilt Assembly Diagram *opposite*, lay out the nine block units, the six tan print 3½×21½" sashing strips, and the four tan print 3½×69½" sashing strips in horizontal rows.

2. Sew together the pieces in each row. Press the seam allowances toward the tan print sashing strips. Join the rows; press.

3. Add a tan print 3½×75½" sashing strip to the side edges of the pieced rows to complete the quilt center. Press the seam allowances toward the strips. The pieced quilt center should measure 75½" square, including the seam allowances.

Add the Pieced Border

1. Sew together one tan print triangle and one rust polka-dot triangle to make a triangle-square (see Diagram 3). Press the seam allowance toward the rust triangle. The pieced triangle-square should measure 3½" square, including the seam allowances. Repeat to make a total of 104 triangle-squares.

Diagram 3

2. Referring to the Quilt Assembly Diagram, join 25 triangle-squares to make the top border strip. Press the seam allowances in one direction. The top border strip should measure 3½×75½", including the seam allowances. Repeat to make the bottom border strip. Sew the pieced border strips to the top and bottom edges of the pieced quilt center.

3. Referring to the Quilt Assembly Diagram, join 27 triangle-squares to make the border strip for the left-hand edge, noting the placement of the triangle-square on the bottom. Press the seam allowances in one direction. The side border strip should measure 3½×81½", including the seam allowances. Repeat to make the border strip for the right-hand edge, noting the placement of the triangle-square on the top. Sew the pieced border strips to the side edges of the pieced quilt center to complete the quilt top. Press all seam allowances toward the pieced border.

Quilt Assembly Diagram

Complete the Quilt

1. Layer the quilt top, batting, and backing according to the instructions in Quilter's Schoolhouse, which begins on *page 150*. Quilt as desired.

2. Use the rust polka-dot 2½×42" strips to bind the quilt according to the instructions in Quilter's Schoolhouse.

Tiger Lily Quilt
optional sizes

If you'd like to make this quilt in a size other than for a large wall hanging, use the information *below*.

Alternate quilt sizes	Small Wall	Full/Queen	King
Number of blocks	16	48	64
Number of block units	4	12	16
Number of block units wide by long	2×2	3×4	4×4
Finished size	57" square	81×105"	105" square
Yardage requirements			
Each of four rust prints	¼ yard	½ yard	⅝ yard
Each of four blue prints	¼ yard	½ yard	⅝ yard
Each of five green prints	¼ yard	⅝ yard	¾ yard
Tan print	3½ yards	7¼ yards	9 yards
Rust polka dot	1⅓ yards	2 yards	2⅜ yards
Backing	3½ yards	7¼ yards	9¼ yards
Batting	63" square	87×111"	111" square

continued

WOOL WALL HANGING

Hand-dyed felted wool in an array of soft colors lends a rich palette to this garden motif and showcases a number of embroidery stitches.

Materials

Scraps of assorted blue, red, purple, pink, orange, and gold felted wools for flower and triangle appliqués

⅝ yard of sage green felted wool for appliqué foundation

⅜ yard of black felted wool for appliqué foundation, triangle appliqués, and binding

⅓ yard of yellow check felted wool for appliqué foundations

⅛ yard total of assorted dark green felted wools for leaf and stem appliqués

1¼ yards of homespun cotton for backing

2 yards of lightweight fusible web

Embroidery floss: gold, black, and green

Freezer paper

Finished wall hanging: 43×21⅛"

About the Wool

Felted wool is a favorite of quilters because its edges won't ravel when cut. The wools used in this project were hand-dyed for a mottled appearance.

To felt wool, machine-wash it in a hot-water-wash, cool-rinse cycle with a small amount of detergent; machine-dry and steam-press.

Cut the Fabrics

To make the best use of your fabrics, cut the pieces in the order that follows. This project uses "Tiger Lily" patterns, which are on *Pattern Sheet 2*. To use freezer paper for cutting the appliqué shapes, as was done in this project, complete the following steps.

1. Place the patterns on a light box and position the freezer paper, shiny side down, over the patterns (see Photo 1). With a pencil, trace the patterns the number of times specified *opposite*, leaving ½" between tracings. Cut out the freezer-paper shapes about ¼" outside the traced lines.

2. Press the freezer-paper shapes onto the right sides of the designated fabrics (see Photo 2); let cool.

3. Cut out the fabric shapes along the solid traced lines, cutting the fabric edges cleanly and smoothly; peel off the freezer paper (see Photo 3).

Photo 1

Photo 2

Photo 3

Photo 4

From assorted blue, red, purple, pink, orange, and gold
wool, cut:

*   17 *each* of patterns A and B
*   13—1" squares

From sage green wool, cut:

*   1—19×43" rectangle for appliqué foundation

From black wool, cut:

*   1—1¼×43" binding strip
*   1—11½" square for appliqué foundation
*   7—3" squares, cutting each in half diagonally for
    a total of 14 triangle appliqués (you'll have
    1 leftover triangle)

From yellow checked wool, cut:

*   2—10" squares for appliqué foundations

From assorted dark green wools, cut:

*   6 of Pattern C
*   14 of Pattern D
*   7 of Pattern E
*   3 *each* of patterns F and G

From homespun, cut:

*   1—19×43" rectangle for backing
*   7—3" squares, cutting each in half diagonally
    for a total of 14 triangles (you'll have
    1 leftover triangle)

From fusible web, cut:

*   1—19×43" rectangle
*   7—3" squares, cutting each in half diagonally
    for a total of 14 triangles (you'll have
    1 leftover triangle)

Appliqué the Flower Blocks

1. Referring to Photo 4, *opposite;* the photograph
    above; and the Wool Wall Hanging Appliqué
    Placement Diagram on *Pattern Sheet 2,* position
    the appliqué shapes on the foundations, layering
    as needed from bottom to top. Baste the leaf,
    stem, and flower appliqué pieces onto the yellow
    check 10" squares and the black 11½" square.

continued

2. Using matching thread, hand-stitch the appliqués in place. Using two strands of green embroidery floss, randomly couch the stems so the wool shows through.

To couch, refer to the diagram *right*. First pull your needle up at A. Insert the needle back into the fabric at B and come up again at C. Continue in this manner along each stem.

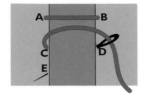

Couching Stitch

3. Stitch the leaves down their centers using a running stitch.

To make a running stitch, refer to the diagram *below*. Pull your needle up at A and insert it back into the fabric at B, ⅛" away from A. Pull your needle up at C, ⅛" from B, and repeat.

Running Stitch

4. Using two strands of gold embroidery floss, cross-stitch along the top edge of the flower bases.

To cross-stitch, refer to the diagram *right*. Pull your needle up at A, then push it down at B. Bring your needle up at C, cross over the first stitch, and push your needle down at D to form an X.

Cross-stitch

Appliqué the Background

1. Referring to the Appliqué Placement Diagram on *Pattern Sheet 2*, position the three appliquéd squares on the sage green 19×43" rectangle and pin in place. Using two strands of black embroidery floss, blanket-stitch the yellow check appliquéd squares in place.

To blanket-stitch, refer to the diagram *right*. First pull your needle up at A, form a reverse L shape

Blanket Stitch

with the floss, and hold the angle of the L shape in place with your thumb. Then push your needle down at B and come up at C to secure the stitch.

2. Using two strands of gold embroidery floss, blanket-stitch the black flower block in place.

3. Referring to the Appliqué Placement Diagram, pin the remaining leaf, stem, and flower appliqué pieces along the bottom edge of the sage green 19×43" rectangle. Hand-stitch in place as before.

Assemble the Quilt

1. Following the manufacturer's instructions, fuse the fusible-web 19×43" rectangle to the wrong side of the homespun 19×43" rectangle; remove the paper backing. Layer the appliquéd rectangle and the homespun; fuse together. Using three strands of black embroidery floss, blanket-stitch together the two side edges and the bottom edges.

2. Referring to the photograph on *page 129* and using two strands of black embroidery floss, quilt ¼" from the edges of the appliquéd squares.

Complete the Quilt

1. Fold the black wool 1¼×43" strip in half lengthwise; press. Open up the strip and place the top edge of the quilt right side up along the fold line. Fold the strip over the edge; pin to the front of the quilt to form the binding. Using one strand of black embroidery floss, whipstitch the front edge of the strip to the quilt. Repeat with the back edge.

2. To make the triangle appliqués, place an assorted wool 1" square on each black triangle so the straight edges are ¼" from the bottom edges and the points are aligned (see Triangle Appliqué Diagram). Using one strand of gold embroidery floss, whipstitch the squares in place. Using two strands of gold embroidery floss, make a cross-stitch in the center of each square.

Triangle Appliqué Diagram

3. Place a fusible-web triangle on the back of an appliquéd triangle; fuse in place. Remove the paper backing. Fuse an appliquéd triangle to each homespun triangle. Using two strands of gold embroidery floss, blanket-stitch around the edges of the triangles.

4. Pin an appliquéd triangle to the center bottom edge of the wall hanging so the raw edges are touching. Overlap the remaining triangles evenly along the wall hanging edge. Using one strand of black embroidery floss, whipstitch each triangle in place. Using a pressing cloth, carefully steam-press. Allow to dry completely.

5. Add a hanging sleeve according to instructions in Quilter's Schoolhouse, which begins on *page 150*.

TOTE BAG

Use fusible web to embellish this practical tote with bright flowers.

Materials

Scraps of yellow, pink, blue, black, and green prints
  for appliqués

Purchased 14×13" canvas tote bag

Heavyweight fusible web

Cut the Fabrics

To make the best use of your fabrics, cut the pieces in the order that follows.

This project uses "Tiger Lily" patterns, which are on *Pattern Sheet 2*. To use fusible web for appliquéing, as was done in this project, complete the following steps.

1. Lay the fusible web, paper side up, over the patterns. With a pencil, trace each pattern the number of times specified *below,* leaving ½" between tracings. Cut out the pieces roughly ¼" outside the traced lines.

2. Following the manufacturer's instructions, press the fusible-web shapes onto the back of the designated fabrics; let cool. Cut out the pieces on the drawn lines. Peel off the paper backings.

From *each* yellow, pink, and blue print, cut:
• 1 of Pattern A
From black print, cut:
• 3 of Pattern B
From green print, cut:
• 2 *each* of patterns C and D
• 1 *each* of patterns E, F, and G

Appliqué the Tote Bag

Referring to the photograph *above,* position the prepared appliqué pieces on the tote bag, working from the bottom piece to the top. Fuse in place.

Serendipity

When she found red and pink prints lying side by side in her stash, designer

Peggy Waltman noticed how good they looked together. She decided to turn them

into a quilt, adding a variety of green prints to complete her palette of pure hues.

Materials

2 yards of white print for blocks and
    outer border
1 yard total of assorted pink prints for blocks, flower
    appliqués, and outer border
1¼ yards of light green print for vine and leaf
    appliqués, blocks, inner border, and outer border
¾ yard total of assorted green prints for blocks,
    leaf appliqués, and outer border

Scrap of lime green imitation suede for
    flower appliqués
1 yard of red print for appliqué foundations
    and sashing
⅝ yard of green polka dot for binding
2⅔ yards of backing fabric
59×48" of quilt batting
Embroidery floss: lime green

Finished quilt top: 52½×42"
Finished block: 7⅛" square

Quantities specified for 44/45"-wide, 100% cotton
fabrics except where noted. All measurements
include a ¼" seam allowance. Sew with right sides
together unless otherwise stated.

continued

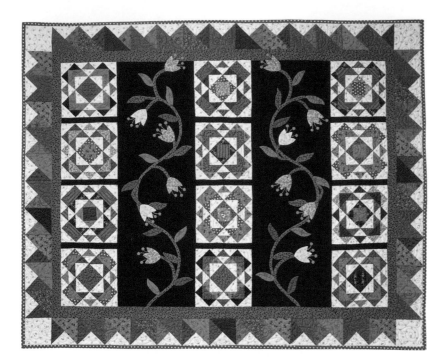

Designer Notes

"My style is happy and crisp. I like to see the difference between light and dark," Peggy Waltman says. "My colors are not wild, [they're] just clear, pure colors."

"Serendipity" started with one block and grew from there. "I like to have a balance of color," Peggy says. "I love trying different color combinations, so I don't use the same fabrics in every square."

Cut the Fabrics

To make the best use of your fabrics, cut the pieces in the order that follows.

The patterns are on *Pattern Sheet 1*. To make templates of the patterns, follow the instructions in Quilter's Schoolhouse, which begins on *page 150.*

From white print, cut:

- 12—4¾" squares for outer border
- 4—4" squares for outer border

From assorted pink prints, cut:

- 24—4⅜" squares for outer border
- 12 of Pattern A

From light green print, cut:

- 3—2⅝×42" strips for inner border
- 2—2×31¼" inner border strips
- 1—18" square, cutting it into enough 1½"-wide bias strips to total 160" in length for vines (For specific instructions, see Cutting Bias Strips in Quilter's Schoolhouse.)

- 3—4¾" squares for outer border
- 2 *each* of patterns B and B reversed

From assorted green prints, cut:

- 12—4¾" squares for outer border
- 11 *each* of patterns B and B reversed

From lime green imitation suede, cut:

- 42 of Pattern C

From red print, cut:

- 2—11¾×33" rectangles for appliqué foundations
- 9—1¼×7⅝" sashing strips

From green polka dot, cut:

- 6—3×42" binding strips

Cut and Assemble the Pink-Center Blocks

Peggy used the same white print in all her blocks; an assortment of pinks and greens gives the quilt a scrappy look. Cutting and piecing instructions for making one block with a pink print center square follow. The pieced pink-center block should measure 7⅝" square, including the seam allowances. Repeat to make a total of six pink-center blocks.

From white print, cut:

- 2—3" squares, cutting each diagonally twice in an X for a total of 8 side triangles
- 4—1¾×3" rectangles
- 2—2¾" squares, cutting each in half diagonally for a total of 4 corner triangles
- 2—2⅛" squares

From pink print No. 1, cut:

- 1—2¼" square

From pink print No. 2, cut:

- 4—1¾×3" rectangles
- 2—2⅛" squares

From green print No. 1, cut:

- 2—2⅛" squares, cutting each in half diagonally for a total of 4 triangles

From green print No. 2, cut:

- 8—1¾" squares

From green print No. 3, cut:

- 8—1¾" squares

1. Sew two green print No. 1 triangles to opposite edges of a pink print No. 1 square (see Diagram 1). Press the seam allowances toward the triangles. Then add green print No. 1 triangles to the remaining edges

Diagram 1

of the square to make the center unit. Press the seam allowances toward the triangles. The pieced center unit should measure 3" square, including the seam allowances.

2. For accurate sewing lines, use a quilter's pencil to mark a diagonal line on the wrong sides of eight green print No. 2 squares, eight green print No. 3 squares, and two white print 2⅛" squares. (To prevent your fabric from stretching as you draw the lines, place 220-grit sandpaper under the squares.)

3. Align a marked green print No. 2 square with one end of a white print 1¾×3" rectangle (see Diagram 2; note the placement of the marked diagonal line). Stitch on the marked line; trim away the excess fabric, leaving a ¼" seam allowance. Press the attached triangle open.

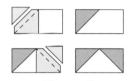

Diagram 2

4. In the same manner, align a second marked green print No. 2 square with the opposite end of the white print rectangle (see Diagram 2, again noting the placement of the marked diagonal line). Stitch on the marked line; trim and press as before to make a white Flying Geese unit. The pieced white Flying Geese unit should still measure 1¾×3", including the seam allowances.

5. Repeat steps 3 and 4 to make a total of four white Flying Geese units. Then use the marked green print No. 3 squares and the pink print 1¾×3" rectangles to make four pink Flying Geese units (see Diagram 3).

Diagram 3

6. Layer each marked white print 2⅛" square atop a pink print No. 2 square (see Diagram 4). Sew each pair together with two seams, stitching ¼" on each side of the drawn lines. Cut each pair apart on its drawn line (see Diagram 5) to make a total of four triangle units. Press the triangle units

open to make four triangle-squares (see Diagram 6). Each pieced triangle-square should measure 1¾" square, including the seam allowances.

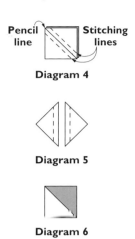

Diagram 4

Diagram 5

Diagram 6

7. Referring to Diagram 7 for placement, lay out the center unit, the four white Flying Geese units, the four pink Flying Geese units, the four triangle-squares, eight white print side triangles, and four white print corner triangles in diagonal rows.

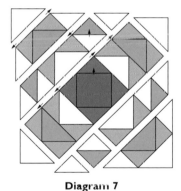

Diagram 7

8. Sew together the pieces in each row. Press the seam allowances as indicated by the arrows in Diagram 7. Then join the rows to make a pink-center block. The pieced pink-center block should measure 7⅝", including the seam allowances. Press the seam allowances in one direction.

Cut and Assemble the Green-Center Blocks

Following are the cutting instructions for making one green-center block. Follow the piecing instructions for Cut and Assemble the Pink-Center Blocks, replacing the pink print pieces with green print pieces and the green print pieces with pink print pieces; refer to Diagram 8 on *page 136* to lay

Serendipity

continued

out the pieces. The pieced green-center block should measure 7⅝" square, including the seam allowances. Repeat to make a total of six green-center blocks.

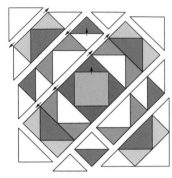

Diagram 8

From white print, cut:
- 2—3" squares, cutting each diagonally twice in an X for a total of 8 side triangles
- 4—1¾×3" rectangles
- 2—2¾" squares, cutting each in half diagonally for a total of 4 corner triangles
- 2—2⅛" squares

From green print No. 1, cut:
- 1—2¼" square

From green print No. 2, cut:
- 4—1¾×3" rectangles
- 2—2⅛" squares

From pink print No. 1, cut:
- 2—2⅛" squares, cutting each in half diagonally for a total of 4 triangles

From pink print No. 2, cut:
- 8—1¾" squares

From pink print No. 3, cut:
- 8—1¾" squares

Appliqué the Foundations

1. Cut and piece the light green print 1½"-wide bias strips to make the following:
   - 2—40"-long strips
   - 12—6"-long strips

2. Fold each light green print strip in half lengthwise with the wrong side inside; press. Stitch ¼" from the long raw edges on each folded strip (see Diagram 9). Trim the seam allowances to ⅛". Refold the strips, centering the seams in the back to make the vine appliqués; press.

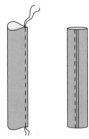

Diagram 9

3. Referring to the Appliqué Placement Diagram, arrange one 40"-long vine appliqué, six 6"-long vine appliqués, five pink print flower appliqués, 13 light green and green print leaf appliqués, and 17 lime green imitation suede circle appliqués on a red print 11¾×33" appliqué foundation. When pleased with the arrangement, baste the pieces in place. *Note:* The remaining appliqué pieces for this foundation will be stitched in place after the inner border is added.

Appliqué Placement Diagram

4. Using thread in colors that match the fabrics, appliqué the pieces to the foundation starting with the bottom pieces.

5. Using three strands of lime green embroidery floss, stem-stitch between each flower and the green imitation suede circles.

To stem-stitch, refer to the diagram *right*. First pull your needle up at A, then insert your needle back into the fabric at B, about ⅜" away from A. Holding the floss out of the way, bring your needle back up at C and pull the floss through so it lies flat against the fabric. The distances between points A, B, and C should be equal. Pull with equal tautness after each stitch. Continue in the same manner to get the desired length.

Stem Stitch

6. Trim the red print appliqué foundation to measure 11¹⁄₁₆×31¼", including the seam allowances, to complete an appliquéd panel.

7. Repeat steps 3 through 6, reversing the placement of the vine and flowers, to make a second appliquéd panel.

Assemble the Quilt Center

1. Referring to the photograph on *page 134*, lay out the 12 pieced blocks, the nine red print 1¼×7⅝" sashing strips, and the two appliquéd panels in vertical rows.

2. Sew together the blocks and sashing strips in three rows. Press the seam allowances toward the sashing strips. Then join the rows and appliquéd panels to make the quilt center. Press the seam allowances toward the appliquéd panels. The pieced quilt center should measure 43×31¼", including the seam allowances.

Add the Inner Border

1. Cut and piece the light green print 2⅝×42" strips to make the following:
   • 2—2⅝×46" inner border strips

2. Sew the light green print 2×31¼" inner border strips to the short edges of the pieced quilt center. Then add the pieced light green print 2⅝×46" inner border strips to the top and bottom edges of the quilt center. Press all seam allowances toward the inner border. The pieced quilt center should now measure 46×35½", including the seam allowances.

3. Appliqué the remaining pink print flower appliqués and lime green imitation suede circles and complete the embroidery on the appliquéd panels.

Assemble and Add the Outer Border

1. Mark a diagonal line on the wrong side of the 12 white print 4¾" squares and the 24 assorted pink print 4⅜" squares.

2. Layer each marked white print 4¾" square atop a green print 4¾" square. Referring to diagrams 4, 5, and 6 on *page 135*, sew each pair together with two seams, stitching ¼" on each side of the drawn lines. Cut each pair apart on its drawn line to

make a total of 24 triangle units. Press the triangle units open to make a total of 24 triangle-squares. Each pieced triangle-square should measure 4⅜" square, including the seam allowances.

3. Align each marked pink print 4⅜" square atop a triangle-square (see Diagram 10; note that the marked diagonal line should be perpendicular to the seam of the triangle-square). Sew each pair together with two seams, stitching ¼" on each side of the drawn lines. Cut the pairs apart on the drawn lines to make a total of 48 triangle units. Press each triangle unit open to make a total of 48 border blocks (you'll have two border blocks leftover). Each pieced border block should measure 4" square, including the seam allowances.

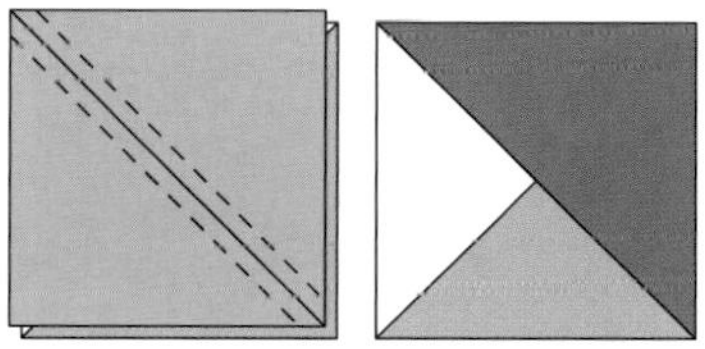

Diagram 10

4. Referring to the photograph on *page 134* for placement, sew together 10 border blocks in a row to make a side border unit. Press the seam allowances in one direction. Repeat to make a second side border unit. Join the side border units to the side edges of the quilt center. Press the seam allowances toward the quilt center.

5. Referring to the photograph, join 13 border blocks in a row; add a white print 4" square to each end of the row to make a top border unit. Press the seam allowances in one direction. Repeat to make a bottom border unit. Join the border units to the top and bottom edges of the pieced quilt center to complete the quilt top; press.

Complete the Quilt

1. Layer the quilt top, batting, and backing according to the instructions in Quilter's Schoolhouse, which begins on *page 150*.

2. Quilt as desired. Peggy chose to hand-quilt continuous swirls and curlicues in a variety of sizes across the quilt top. To add interest, she accented the end of each curlicue with a French knot (see photo on *page 138*). "When you're hand-quilting, don't get stressed out about the

continued

stitch size," Peggy says. "Just try it. It's relaxing. You can individualize the quilt as you go."

Peggy does not use a hoop when hand-quilting. She bastes everything, then uses appliqué pins to secure the space she plans to stitch. "Then you can take the quilt with you wherever you go," Peggy says.

3. Use the green polka-dot 3×42" strips to bind the quilt according to the instructions in Quilter's Schoolhouse.

BED QUILT

Purple and blue flowers cascade down between panels of floral fabric in this full-size quilt.

No borders to cut or sew simplify the quilt's design.

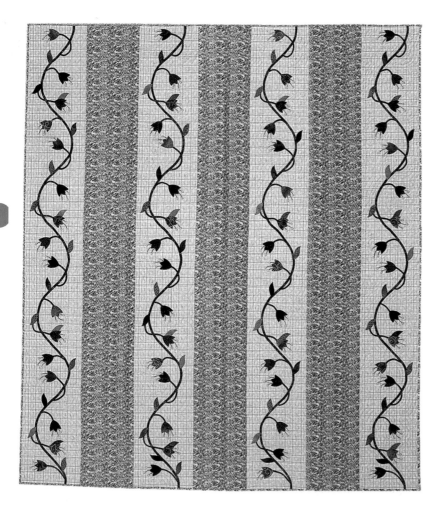

Materials

4¾ yards of green plaid for appliqué foundations

3⅛ yards of purple-and-green print for sashing
 and binding

½ yard total of assorted purple and blue prints
 for flower appliqués

1¼ yards of green print for vine and stem appliqués

⅜ yard total of assorted green prints
 for leaf appliqués

⅛ yard of gold print for circle appliqués

5 yards of backing fabric

81×90" of quilt batting

Embroidery floss: green

Finished quilt top: 75×84"

Cut the Fabrics

To make the best use of your fabrics, cut the pieces in the order that follows.

This project uses "Serendipity" patterns, which are on *Pattern Sheet 1.*

The appliqué foundation strips and sashing strips are cut the length of the fabric (parallel to the selvage).

From green plaid, cut:
- 4—11¾×84½" strips for appliqué foundations

From purple-and-green print, cut:
- 3—10½×84½" sashing strips
- 9—2½×42" binding strips

From assorted purple and blue prints, cut:
- 64 of Pattern A

From green print, cut:
- 1—24×42" rectangle, cutting it into enough 1½"-wide bias strips to total 400" in length for vines (For specific instructions, see Cutting Bias Strips in Quilter's Schoolhouse, which begins on *page 150.*)
- 1—18×42" rectangle, cutting it into enough 1"-wide bias strips to total 300" in length for stems

From assorted green prints, cut:
- 32 *each* of patterns B and B reversed

From gold print, cut:
- 192 of Pattern C

Appliqué the Foundations

1. Cut and piece the green print 1½"-wide bias strips to make the following:
- 4—100"-long strips

2. Cut and piece the green print 1"-wide bias strips to make the following:
- 16—7"-long strips
- 12—5"-long strips
- 20—4"-long strips
- 16—3"-long strips

3. Referring to Appliqué the Foundations on *page 136,* Step 2, prepare the vine and stem appliqués.

4. Referring to the photograph *opposite,* arrange one 100"-long vine strip, four 7"-long stem strips, three 5"-long stem strips, five 4"-long stem strips, and four 3"-long stem strips on a green plaid 11¾×84½" appliqué foundation strip. Also arrange 16 purple and blue print flower appliqués, 16 green print leaf appliqués, and 48 gold print circle appliqués on the green plaid foundation strip. Baste the pieces in place. Referring to steps 4 and 5 on *page 136,* complete the appliqué and

embroidery. Appliqué the remaining green plaid 11¾×84½" foundation strips in the same manner.

Assemble the Quilt Center

Lay out the four appliquéd strips and the three purple-and-green print sashing strips; sew together to make the quilt top. The pieced quilt top should measure 75½×84½", including the seam allowances.

Complete the Quilt

1. Layer the quilt top, batting, and backing according to the instructions in Quilter's Schoolhouse, which begins on *page 150.* Quilt as desired.

2. Use the purple-and-green print 2½×42" strips to bind the quilt according to the instructions in Quilter's Schoolhouse.

Serendipity

WALL QUILT

Turn the pieced block border from the

"Serendipity" pattern into this charming

small quilt for a wall or tabletop.

Materials

⅞ yard of red floral for blocks and outer border

⅞ yard of red stripe for blocks, sashing, inner border, and binding

⅝ yard of blue print for blocks

1⅞ yards of backing fabric

45" square of quilt batting

Finished quilt top: 39" square
Finished block: 7" square

Cut the Fabrics

To make the best use of your fabrics, cut the pieces in the order that follows.

From red floral, cut:
• 2—4½×31½" outer border strips
• 2—4½×39½" outer border strips
• 16—4¾" squares
• 1—1½" square

From red stripe, cut:
• 4—2½×42" binding strips
• 2—1½×31½" inner border strips
• 2—1½×29½" inner border strips
• 4—1½×14½" sashing strips
• 16—4¾" squares

From blue print, cut:
• 32—4⅜" squares

Assemble the Blocks

1. Referring to Assemble and Add the Outer Border on *page 137*, steps 1 through 3, use the 16 red floral 4¾" squares, the 16 red stripe 4¾" squares, and the 32 blue print 4⅜" squares to make 32 of Block Unit A and 32 of Block Unit B (see Diagram 1).

Block Unit A   **Block Unit B**

Diagram 1

2. Sew together four of Block Unit A in pairs (see Diagram 2). Press the seam allowances in opposite directions. Then join the pairs to make

a Pinwheel block. The pieced Pinwheel block should measure 7½" square, including the seam allowances. Repeat to make a total of eight Pinwheel blocks.

Diagram 2

3. Sew together four Pinwheel blocks in pairs (see Diagram 3). Press the seam allowances in opposite directions. Then join the pairs to make a block unit. Press the seam allowance in one direction. The block unit should measure 14½" square, including the seam allowances. Repeat to make a total of two block units.

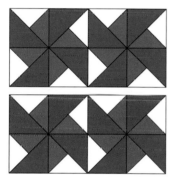

Diagram 3

4. Using Block Unit B, repeat Step 2 to make a total of eight Pinwheel blocks (see Diagram 4). Repeat Step 3 to make a total of two block units.

Diagram 4

Assemble the Quilt Center

1. Referring to the photograph *right* for placement, lay out the four red stripe 1½x14½" sashing strips, the red floral 1½" square, and the four block units in horizontal rows.

2. Sew together the pieces in each row. Press the seam allowances toward the sashing strips. Then join the rows to make the quilt center. Press the seam allowances in one direction. The pieced quilt center should measure 29½" square, including the seam allowances.

Add the Borders

1. Sew the red stripe 1½x29½" inner border strips to opposite edges of the quilt center. Add the red stripe 1½x31½" inner border strips to the remaining edges of the quilt center. Press the seam allowances toward the inner border.

2. Sew the red floral 4½x31½" outer border strips to opposite edges of the quilt center. Then join the red floral 4½x39½" outer border strips to the remaining edges of the quilt center to complete the quilt top. Press all seam allowances toward the outer border.

Complete the Quilt

1. Layer the quilt top, batting, and backing according to the instructions in Quilter's Schoolhouse, which begins on *page 150*. Quilt as desired.

2. Use the red stripe 2½x42" strips to bind the quilt according to the instructions in Quilter's Schoolhouse.

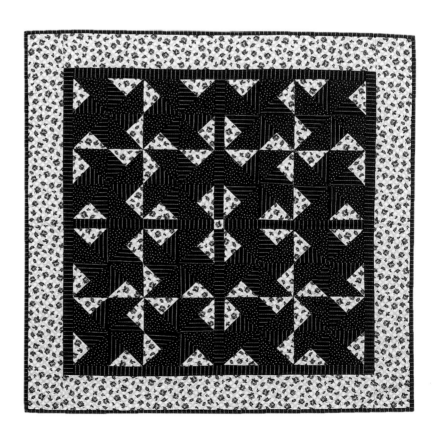

SWEET *Lullabies*

Peggy Kotek used an 1850s baby quilt as inspiration when designing this small appliqué album quilt, which she uses to teach beginning quilters.

Materials

2 yards of cream print for appliqué foundations,
   sashing, borders, and binding

1/3 yard of pink print for appliqués

1/8 yard of solid pink for appliqués

1/2 yard of solid green for appliqués and
   sawtooth border

Scrap of light green print for appliqués

1 1/8 yards of backing fabric

41" square of quilt batting

Embroidery floss: green

Freezer paper

Finished quilt top: 35" square
Finished block: 10" square

Quantities specified for 44/45"-wide, 100% cotton fabrics. All measurements include a ¼" seam allowance. Sew with right sides together unless otherwise stated.

Cut the Fabrics

To make the best use of your fabrics, cut the pieces in the order that follows. The patterns are on *Pattern Sheet 2*. To make templates of the patterns, follow the instructions in Quilter's Schoolhouse, which begins on *page 150*. For Pattern H, follow steps 1 and 2 under Cut and Appliqué the Fleur-de-Lis Block on *page 145* to trace a complete template.

To use the freezer-paper appliqué method, as was used in this project, complete the steps on *page 144*.

continued

1. Position the freezer paper, shiny side down, over all patterns except H. Trace each pattern once. Cut out the freezer-paper templates on the lines.

2. Press the freezer-paper templates onto the right sides of the designated fabrics; let cool.

3. Cut out the fabric shapes, adding a ³⁄₁₆" seam allowance. Remove the template and reuse.

From cream print, cut:
- 4—2×42" binding strips
- 2—4½×35½" outer border strips
- 2—4½×27½" outer border strips
- 2—2×24½" inner border strips
- 2—2×21½" inner border strips
- 1—1½×21½" sashing strip
- 4—10½" squares for appliqué foundations
- 2—1½×10½" sashing strips
- 33—2⅜" squares, cutting each in half diagonally for a total of 66 triangles
- 2—2" squares for sawtooth border

From pink print, cut:
- 1—10½" square for Pattern H
- 4 of Pattern A

From solid pink, cut:
- 13 of Pattern G
- 1 of Pattern J

From solid green, cut:
- 33—2⅜" squares, cutting each in half diagonally for a total of 66 triangles
- 12 of Pattern C
- 4 *each* of patterns D and I
- 1 of Pattern E
- 10 of Pattern F

From light green print, cut:
- 4 of Pattern B
- 1 of Pattern K

Appliqué the Rose Block

1. Referring to the Rose Block Appliqué Placement Diagram, arrange the four pink print A roses, the four light green print B rose centers, the 12 solid green C leaves, and the four solid green D stems on a cream print 10½" square appliqué foundation. Baste in place.

2. Using green thread, appliqué the leaves to the foundation, starting each one at a stem's edge so all leaves touch a stem. Appliqué the remaining pieces in place using matching threads.

Rose Block Appliqué Placement Diagram

Appliqué the Cherry Wreath Block

1. To make templates for the cherries, trace Pattern G 13 times on lightweight card stock; cut out. Baste around the edge of each solid pink G cherry and gather each one around a card-stock template; press. When cool, cut threads and remove the templates.

2. Referring to the Cherry Wreath Block Appliqué Placement Diagram, arrange the solid green E ring, the 10 solid green F leaves, and the 13 solid pink G cherries on a cream print 10½" square appliqué foundation. Baste in place.

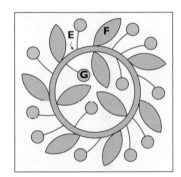

Cherry Wreath Block Appliqué Placement Diagram

3. Clip the inside edge of the seam allowance of the solid green E ring; using green thread, appliqué the ring to the foundation, sewing the inside edge first.

4. Using green thread, appliqué the leaves to the foundation, starting each one at the ring's edge so all leaves will touch the ring.

5. Using two strands of green embroidery floss, stem-stitch the 13 cherry stems.

   To stem-stitch, refer to the diagram *opposite*. Pull your needle up at A, then insert your needle back into the fabric at B, about ⅜" away from A. Holding the floss out of the way, bring your needle back up at C and pull the floss through so it lies flat against the fabric. The distances between points A, B, and C should be equal. Pull with equal tautness after each stitch. Continue in the same manner to reach your desired length.

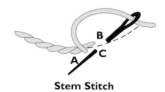

Stem Stitch

6. Appliqué each cherry to the foundation.

Appliqué the Leaf Block

1. Referring to the Leaf Block Appliqué Placement Diagram, arrange the four solid green I leaves, the solid pink J bud, and the light green print K bud center on a cream print 10½" square appliqué foundation. Baste in place.

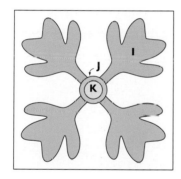

**Leaf Block Appliqué
Placement Diagram**

2. Using threads that match the fabrics, appliqué the pieces to the foundation.

Cut and Appliqué the Fleur-de-Lis Block

Designer Peggy Kotek used freezer paper and needle-turn appliqué to create this block. The pattern piece is cut out as it is appliquéd to the foundation. The steps are as follows.

1. Cut a 10½" square of freezer paper. Fold the freezer-paper square in half horizontally with the shiny side inside, then fold it in half again vertically; crease the folds.

2. Unfold the freezer paper and align adjacent horizontal and vertical crease lines with the dashed lines on Pattern H (Quarter Pattern); trace Pattern H. Refold the freezer paper. Pin or staple the layers so they won't move while being cut. Cut out the design on the solid traced lines, including the center area, to make a freezer-paper template. Remove the pins or staples.

3. Carefully unfold the freezer-paper template and center it, shiny side down, on the right side of the pink print 10½" square. Using a dry iron set on cotton, press the freezer paper to the fabric. Trace the outline of the template with a fabric marker, making sure every part of the design is traced. (The marks need to be visible throughout the appliqué process.) Remove the freezer-paper template, but do not cut out the appliqué piece.

4. With right sides up, place the marked pink print square on the remaining cream print 10½" square appliqué foundation, aligning the fabrics' straight edges. Baste the squares together. The basting should hold the design in place until appliquéing is complete and should not be too close to the areas where you'll do your needle-turn stitching.

5. Cut out a small portion of the appliqué design at a time (about 1"), cutting a scant ³⁄₁₆" away from the drawn lines so the lines can be your turn-under guide. Be careful not to cut the foundation fabric. Snip deeply only if inside a curve, and then sparingly. By cutting a little at a time, the piece remains more stable. Appliqué the portion in place with small blind stitches and pink thread, turning the edge under with your needle as you work. Continue in the same manner until the entire fleur-de-lis is appliquéd to the foundation.

Assemble the Quilt Center

1. Referring to the photograph on *page 143* for placement, lay out the four appliquéd blocks, the two cream print 1½×10½" sashing strips, and the cream print 1½×21½" sashing strip in horizontal rows.

2. Sew together the pieces in each row. Press the seam allowances toward the sashing strips. Join the rows to make the quilt center. The pieced quilt center should measure 21½" square, including the seam allowances.

continued

Add the Borders

1. Sew the cream print 2×21½" inner border strips to opposite edges of the pieced quilt center. Add the cream print 2×24½" inner border strips to the remaining edges of the pieced quilt center. Press the seam allowances toward the inner border.

2. Sew together one cream print triangle and one solid green triangle to make a triangle-square (see Triangle-Square Diagram). Press the seam allowance toward the green triangle. The triangle-square should measure 2" square, including the seam allowances. Repeat to make a total of 66 triangle-squares.

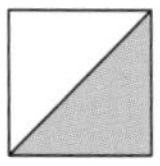

Triangle-Square Diagram

3. Referring to the photograph on *page 143*, sew together 16 triangle-squares to make a short sawtooth border unit; press. Repeat to make a second short sawtooth border unit. Sew the border units to opposite edges of the pieced quilt center. Press the seam allowances toward the cream print inner border.

4. Sew together 17 triangle-squares and one cream print 2" square to make a long sawtooth border unit; press. Repeat to make a second long sawtooth border unit. Join the units to the remaining edges of the pieced quilt center. Press the seam allowances toward the inner border.

5. Sew the cream print 4½×27½" outer border strips to opposite edges of the pieced quilt center. Then add the cream print 4½×35½" outer border strips to the remaining edges of the pieced quilt center to complete the quilt top. Press all seam allowances toward the outer border.

Complete the Quilt

1. Layer the quilt top, batting, and backing according to the instructions in Quilter's Schoolhouse, which begins on *page 150*.

2. Quilt as desired. Peggy hand-quilted around each appliqué motif, then filled the background with diagonal stitching.

3. Use the cream print 2×42" strips to bind the quilt according to the instructions in Quilter's Schoolhouse.

Sweet Lullabies Quilt
optional sizes

If you'd like to make this quilt in a size other than for a wall quilt, use the information *below*.

Alternate quilt sizes	Throw	Full/Queen	King
Number of blocks	24	56	64
Number of blocks wide by long	4×6	7×8	8×8
Number of each pattern	6	14	16
Number of triangle-squares	154	228	242
Finished short inner border width	1¼"	1½"	1½"
Finished long inner border width	1¾"	1¾"	1½"
Finished size	57½×78½"	90½×101"	101" square
Yardage requirements			
Cream print	4½ yards	8 yards	9 yards
Pink print	⅞ yard	1¾ yards	1⅞ yards
Solid pink	¼ yard	⅜ yard	½ yard
Solid green	1⅝ yards	3¼ yards	3½ yards
Light green print	⅛ yard	¼ yard	¼ yard
Backing	4¾ yards	8⅛ yards	9 yards
Batting	64×85"	97×107"	107" square

APPLIQUÉD COAT

Add color and personality to any denim garment or accessory with hand-dyed felted wool.

Materials

Scraps of assorted red and light green felted wool

⅛ yard of dark green felted wool

Purchased denim coat

Lightweight fusible web

About the Wool

Felted wool is a favorite of quilters because its edges won't ravel when cut. The wools used in this project were hand-dyed for a mottled appearance.

To felt wool, machine-wash it in a hot-water-wash, cool-rinse cycle with a small amount of detergent; machine-dry and steam-press.

Cut the Fabrics

To make the best use of your fabrics, cut the pieces in the order that follows.

This project uses "Sweet Lullabies" patterns F and G, which are on *Pattern Sheet 2*. To use fusible web for appliquéing, as was done in this project, complete the following steps.

1. Lay the fusible web, paper side up, over patterns F and G. With a pencil, trace each pattern the number of times specified *right*, leaving ½" between tracings. Cut out the pieces roughly ¼" outside the traced lines.

2. Following the manufacturer's instructions, press the fusible-web pieces onto the backs of the designated fabrics; let cool. Cut out the fabric pieces on the drawn lines. Peel off the paper backings.

From assorted red wool, cut:
* 24 of Pattern G

From assorted light green wool, cut:
* 15 of Pattern F
* 24—⅜×1¼" strips for stem appliqués

From dark green wool, cut:
* ⅜"-wide strips, enough to make the following lengths for vine appliqués: 1½", 2", 12", 14", and 24"

Appliqué the Coat

1. Referring to the photograph *above*, position the vine and stem appliqué strips on the coat. Baste in place. Then position the prepared appliqué pieces on the coat, working from the bottom layer to the top. Fuse in place.

2. Using color-coordinated embroidery threads, machine-blanket-stitch around each appliqué piece.

BED QUILT

This machine-appliqued fleur-de-lis block,

pulled from the "Sweet Lullabies" quilt,

makes a brilliant splash in bright batiks.

Materials

6—⅓-yard pieces of assorted light batiks in yellow, coral, peach, and green for appliqué foundations

24—11" squares of medium to dark batiks in green, purple, red, orange, and gold for appliqués

1⅛ yards of yellow-green batik for sashing and inner border

¾ yard of multicolor batik for sashing, border corners, and binding

1¾ yards of blue-green batik for outer border

5⅛ yards of backing fabric

68×91" of quilt batting

7 yards of fusible web

Finished quilt top: 61½×84½"

Cut the Fabrics

To make the best use of your fabrics, cut the pieces in the order that follows. This project uses "Sweet Lullabies" Pattern H, which is on *Pattern Sheet 2*.

To use fusible web for appliquéing, as was done in this project, complete the following steps.

1. Referring to Cut and Appliqué the Fleur de-Lis Block on *page 145*, steps 1 and 2, lay the fusible web, paper side up, over Pattern H. Use a pencil to trace the pattern 24 times, leaving ½" between tracings. Cut out each fusible-web piece roughly ¼" outside the traced lines.

2. Following the manufacturer's instructions, press the fusible-web pieces onto the backs of the designated fabrics; let cool. Cut out the fabric shapes on the drawn lines. Peel off the paper backings.

From assorted light batiks, cut:
- 24—10½" squares for appliqué foundations

From assorted medium to dark batiks, cut:
- 24 of Pattern H

From yellow-green batik, cut:
- 6—2×42" strips for inner border
- 38—2×10½" sashing strips

From multicolor batik, cut:
- 8—2½×42" binding strips
- 19—2" squares

From blue-green batik, cut:
- 7—7½×42" strips for outer border

Appliqué the Blocks

1. Position a batik H fleur-de-lis atop each assorted light batik 10½" square appliqué foundation; fuse in place.

2. Using color-coordinated embroidery threads, machine-satin-stitch the pieces to the foundations to make 24 fleur-de-lis blocks.

Assemble the Quilt Center

1. Referring to the photograph *right*, lay out the fleur-de-lis blocks, the yellow-green batik 2×10½" sashing strips, and 15 multicolor batik 2" squares in horizontal rows.

2. Sew together the pieces in each row. Press the seam allowances toward the sashing strips. Join the rows to make the quilt center. Press the seam allowances in one direction. The pieced quilt center should measure 45×68", including the seam allowances.

Add the Borders

1. Cut and piece the yellow-green batik 2×42" strips to make the following:
   - 2—2×68" inner border strips
   - 2—2×45" inner border strips

2. Sew the short inner border strips to the top and bottom edges of the pieced quilt center. Add a multicolor batik 2" square to each end of the long inner border strips. Add the pieced long inner border strips to the side edges of the quilt center. Press the seam allowances toward the inner border.

3. Cut and piece the blue-green batik 7½×42" strips to make the following:
   - 2—7½×85" outer border strips
   - 2—7½×48" outer border strips

4. Join the short outer border strips to the top and bottom edges of the quilt center. Then join the long outer border strips to the side edges of the quilt center to complete the quilt top. Press the seam allowances toward the outer border.

Complete the Quilt

1. Layer the quilt top, batting, and backing according to the instructions in Quilter's Schoolhouse, which begins on *page 150*. Quilt as desired.

2. Use the multicolor batik 2½×42" strips to bind the quilt according to the instructions in Quilter's Schoolhouse.

QUILTER'S SCHOOLHOUSE

GETTING STARTED

Before you begin any project, collect the tools and materials

you'll need in one place.

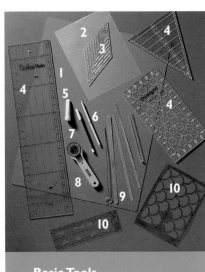

Tools

CUTTING

Acrylic ruler: To aid in making perfectly straight cuts with a rotary cutter, choose a ruler of thick, clear plastic. Many sizes are available. A 6×24" ruler marked in ¼" increments with 30°, 45°, and 60° angles is a good first purchase.

Rotary-cutting mat: A rotary cutter should always be used with a mat designed specifically for it. In addition to protecting the table, the mat helps keep the fabric from shifting while you cut. Often these mats are described as self-healing, meaning the blade does not leave slash marks or grooves in the surface, even after repeated usage. While many shapes and styles are available, a 16×23" mat marked with a 1" grid, with hash marks at ⅛" increments and 45° and 60° angles is a good choice.

Rotary cutter: The round blade of a rotary cutter will cut up to six layers of fabric at once. Because the blade is so sharp, be sure to purchase one with a safety guard and keep the guard over the blade when you're not cutting. The blade can be removed from the handle and replaced when it gets dull. Commonly available in three sizes, a good first blade is a 45 mm.

Scissors: You'll need one pair for cutting fabric and another for cutting paper and plastic.

Pencils and other marking tools: Marks made with special quilt markers are easy to remove after sewing.

Template plastic: This slightly frosted plastic comes in sheets about ¹⁄₁₆" thick.

PIECING

Iron and ironing board

Sewing thread: Use 100-percent-cotton thread.

Sewing machine: Any machine in good working order with well-adjusted tension will produce pucker-free patchwork seams.

APPLIQUÉ

Fusible web: Instead of the traditional method, secure cutout shapes to the background of an appliqué block with this iron-on adhesive.

Hand-sewing needles: For hand appliqué, most quilters like fine quilting needles.

HAND QUILTING

Frame or hoop: You'll get smaller, more even stitches if you stretch your quilt as you stitch. A frame supports the quilt's weight, ensures even tension, and frees both your hands for stitching. However, once set up,

Basic Tools
1. Rotary-cutting mat
2. Template plastic
3. Template
4. Acrylic rulers
5. Chalk marker
6. Marking pencil
7. Water-erasable marker
8. Rotary cutter
9. Bias bars
10. Quilting stencils

it cannot be disassembled until the quilting is complete. Quilting hoops are more portable and less expensive.

Quilting needles: A "between" or quilting needle is short with a small eye. Common sizes are 8, 9, and 10; size 8 is best for beginners.

Quilting thread: Quilting thread is stronger than sewing thread.

Thimble: This finger cover relieves the pressure required to push a needle through several layers of fabric and batting.

MACHINE QUILTING

Darning foot: You may find this tool, also called a hopper foot, in your sewing machine's accessory kit. If not, have the model and brand of your machine available when you go to purchase one. It is used for free-motion stitching.

Safety pins: They hold the layers together during quilting.

Table: Use a large work surface that's level with your machine bed.

Thread: Use 100-percent-cotton quilting thread, cotton-wrapped polyester quilting thread, or fine nylon monofilament thread.

Walking foot: This sewing-machine accessory helps you keep long, straight quilting lines smooth and pucker-free.

Choose Your Fabrics

It is no surprise that most quilters prefer 100-percent-cotton fabrics for quiltmaking. Cotton fabric minimizes seam distortion, presses crisply, and is easy to quilt. Most patterns, including those in this book, specify quantities for 44/45"-wide fabrics unless otherwise noted. Our projects call for a little extra yardage in length to allow for minor errors and slight shrinkage.

Prepare Your Fabrics

There are conflicting opinions about the need to prewash fabric. The debate is a modern one because most antique quilts were made with unwashed fabric. However, the dyes and sizing used today are unlike those used a century ago.

Prewashing fabric offers quilters certainty as its main advantage. Today's fabrics resist bleeding and shrinkage, but some of both can occur in some fabrics—an unpleasant prospect once you've assembled a quilt. Some quilters find prewashed fabric easier to quilt. If you choose to prewash your fabric, press it well before cutting.

Other quilters prefer the crispness of unwashed fabric, especially for machine piecing. And, if you use fabrics with the same fiber content throughout a quilt, then any shrinkage that occurs in its first washing should be uniform. Some quilters find this small amount of shrinkage desirable, since it gives a quilt a slightly puckered, antique look.

We recommend you prewash a scrap of each fabric to test it for shrinkage and bleeding. If you choose to prewash an entire fabric piece, unfold it to a single layer. Wash it in warm water, which will allow the fabric to shrink and/or bleed. If the fabric bleeds, rinse it until the water runs clear. Do not use it in a quilt if it hasn't stopped bleeding. Hang the fabric to dry, or tumble it in the dryer until slightly damp; press well.

Select the Batting

For a small beginner project, a thin cotton batting is a good choice. It has a tendency to "stick" to fabric so it requires less basting. Also, it's easy to stitch. It's wise to follow the stitch density (distance between rows of stitching required to keep the batting from shifting and wadding up inside the quilt) recommendation printed on the packaging.

Polyester batting is lightweight and readily available. In general, it springs back to its original height when compressed, adding a puffiness to quilts. It tends to "beard" (work out between the weave of the fabric) more than natural fibers. Polyester fleece is denser and works well for pillow tops and place mats.

Wool batting has good loft retention and absorbs moisture, making it ideal for cool, damp climates. Read the label carefully before purchasing a wool batting because it may require special handling.

ROTARY CUTTING

We've taken the guesswork out of rotary cutting with this primer.

Plan for Cutting

Quilt-Lovers' Favorites™ instructions list pieces in the order in which they should be cut to make the best use of your fabrics. Always consider the fabric grain before cutting. The arrow on a pattern piece or template indicates which direction the fabric grain should run. One or more straight sides of the pattern piece or template should follow the fabric's lengthwise or crosswise grain.

The lengthwise grain, parallel to the selvage (the tightly finished edge), has the least amount of stretch. (Do not use the selvage of a woven fabric in a quilt. When washed, it may shrink more than the rest of the fabric.) Crosswise grain, perpendicular to the selvage, has a little more give. The edge of any pattern piece that will be on the outside of a block or quilt should always be cut on the lengthwise grain. Be sure to press the fabric before cutting to remove any wrinkles or folds.

Using a Rotary Cutter

When cutting, keep an even pressure on the rotary cutter and make sure the blade is touching the edge of the ruler.

continued

The less you move your fabric when cutting, the more accurate you'll be.

SQUARING UP THE FABRIC EDGE

Before rotary-cutting fabric into strips, it is imperative that one fabric edge be made straight, or squared up. Since all subsequent cuts will be measured from this straight edge, squaring up the fabric edge is an important step. There are several different techniques for squaring up an edge, some of which involve the use of a pair of rulers. For clarity and simplicity, we have chosen to describe a single-ruler technique here. *Note:* The instructions are for right-handers.

1. Lay your fabric on the rotary mat with the right side down and one selvage edge away from you. Fold the fabric with the wrong side inside and the selvages together. Fold the fabric in half again, lining up the fold with the selvage edges. Lightly hand-crease all of the folds.

2. Position the folded fabric on the cutting mat with the selvage edges away from you and the bulk of the fabric length to your left. With the ruler on top of the fabric, align a horizontal grid line on the ruler with the lower folded fabric edge, leaving about 1" of fabric exposed along the right-hand edge of the ruler (see Photo 1). Do not worry about or try to align the uneven raw edges along the right-hand side of the fabric. *Note:* If the grid lines on the cutting mat interfere with your ability to focus on the ruler grid lines, turn your cutting mat over and work on the unmarked side.

3. Hold the ruler firmly in place with your left hand, keeping your fingers away from the right-hand edge and spreading your fingers apart slightly. Apply pressure to the ruler with your fingertips to prevent it from slipping as you cut. With the ruler firmly in place, hold the rotary cutter so the blade is touching the right-hand edge of the ruler. Roll the blade along the ruler edge, beginning just off the folded edge and pushing the cutter away from you, toward the selvage edge.

4. The fabric strip to the right of the ruler's edge should be cut cleanly away, leaving you with a straight edge from which you can measure all subsequent cuts. Do not pick up the fabric once the edge is squared; instead, turn the cutting mat to rotate the fabric and begin cutting strips.

CUTTING AND SUBCUTTING STRIPS

To use a rotary cutter to its greatest advantage, first cut a strip of fabric, then subcut the strip into specific sizes. For example, if your instructions say to cut forty 2" squares, follow these steps.

1. First cut a 2"-wide strip crosswise on the fabric. Assuming you have squared up the fabric edge as described earlier, you can turn your cutting mat clockwise 180° with the newly squared-up edge on your left and the excess fabric on the right. Place the ruler on top of the fabric.

2. Align the 2" grid mark on the ruler with the squared-up edge of the fabric (see Photo 2). *Note:* Align only the vertical grid mark and the fabric raw edge; ignore the selvages at the lower edge that may not line up perfectly with the horizontal ruler grid. A good rule of thumb to remember when rotary-cutting fabric is "the piece you want to keep should be under the ruler." That way, if you accidentally swerve away from the ruler when cutting, the piece under the ruler will be "safe."

3. Placing your rotary cutter along the ruler's right-hand edge and holding the ruler firmly with your left hand, run the blade along the ruler, as in Step 3 of Squaring Up the Fabric Edge, *left,* to cut the strip. Remove the ruler.

4. Sliding the excess fabric out of the way, carefully turn the mat so the 2" strip is horizontal in relation to you. Refer to Squaring Up the Fabric Edge to trim off the selvage edges and square up the strip's short edges.

5. Then align the ruler's 2" grid mark with a squared-up short edge of the strip (the 2" square you want to keep should be under the ruler). Hold the

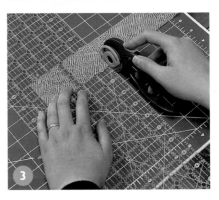

ruler with your left hand and run the rotary cutter along the right-hand ruler edge to cut a 2" square. You can cut multiple 2" squares from one strip by sliding the ruler over 2" from the previous cutting line and cutting again (see Photo 3). From a 44/45"-wide strip, you'll likely be able to cut twenty-one 2" squares. Since in this example you need a total of 40, cut a second 2"-wide strip and subcut it into 2" squares.

CUTTING TRIANGLES

Right triangles also can be quickly and accurately cut with a rotary cutter. There are two common ways to cut triangles. An example of each method follows.

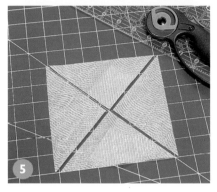

To cut two triangles from one square, the instructions may read:

From green print, cut:
- 20—3" squares, cutting each in half diagonally for a total of 40 triangles

1. Referring to Cutting and Subcutting Strips on *page 152*, cut a 3"-wide fabric strip and subcut the strip into 3" squares.

2. Line up the ruler's edge with opposite corners of a square to cut it in half diagonally (see Photo 4). Cut along the ruler's edge. *Note:* The triangles' resultant long edges are on the bias. Avoid stretching or overhandling these edges when piecing so that seams don't become wavy and distorted.

To cut four triangles from one square, the instructions may read:

From green print, cut:
- 20—6" squares, cutting each diagonally twice in an X for a total of 80 triangles

3. Referring to Cutting and Subcutting Strips on *page 152,* cut a 6"-wide fabric strip and subcut it into 6" squares.

4. Line up the ruler's edge with opposite corners of a square to cut it in half diagonally. Cut along the ruler's edge; do not separate the two triangles created. Line up the ruler's edge with the remaining corners and cut along the ruler's edge to make a total of four triangles (see Photo 5). *Note:* The triangles' resultant short edges are on the bias. Avoid stretching or overhandling these edges when piecing so that seams don't become wavy and distorted.

CUTTING WITH TEMPLATES

A successful quilt requires precise cutting of pieces.

About Scissors

Sharp scissor blades are vital to accurate cutting, but keeping them sharp is difficult because each use dulls the edges slightly. Cutting paper and plastic speeds the dulling process, so invest in a second pair for those materials and reserve your best scissors for fabric.

Make the Templates

For some quilts, you'll need to cut out the same shape multiple times. For accurate piecing later, the individual pieces should be identical to one another.

A template is a pattern made from extra-sturdy material so you can trace around it many times without wearing away the edges. You can make your own templates by duplicating printed patterns (like those on the Pattern Sheets) on plastic.

To make permanent templates, we recommend using easy-to-cut template plastic. This material lasts indefinitely, and its transparency allows you to trace the pattern directly onto its surface.

To make a template, lay the plastic over a printed pattern. Trace the pattern onto the plastic using a ruler and a permanent marker. This will ensure straight lines, accurate corners, and permanency. *Note:* If the pattern you are tracing is a half-pattern to begin with, you must first make a full-size pattern. To do so, fold a piece of tracing paper in half and crease; unfold. Lay the tracing paper over the half-pattern, aligning the crease with the fold line indicated on the pattern. Trace the half-pattern. Then rotate the tracing paper, aligning the half-pattern on the opposite side of the crease to trace the other half of the pattern. Use this full size pattern to create your template.

For hand piecing and appliqué, make templates the exact size of the finished pieces, without seam allowances, by tracing the patterns' dashed lines. For machine piecing, make templates with the seam allowances included.

For easy reference, mark each template with its letter designation, grain line if noted, and block name. Verify the template's size by placing it over the printed pattern. Templates must be accurate or the error, however small, will compound many times as you assemble the quilt. To check the accuracy of your templates, make a test block before cutting the fabric pieces for an entire quilt.

continued

Trace the Templates

To mark on fabric, use a special quilt marker that makes a thin, accurate line. Do not use a ballpoint or ink pen that may bleed if washed. Test all marking tools on a fabric scrap before using them.

To trace pieces that will be used for hand piecing or appliqué, place templates facedown on the wrong side of the fabric; position the tracings at least ½" apart (see Diagram 1, template A). The lines drawn on the fabric are the sewing lines. Mark cutting lines, or estimate by eye a seam allowance around each piece as you cut out the pieces. For hand piecing, add a ¼" seam allowance when cutting out the pieces; for hand appliqué, add a ³⁄₁₆" seam allowance.

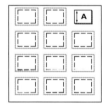

Diagram 1

Templates used to make pieces for machine piecing have seam allowances included so you can use common lines for efficient cutting. To trace, place templates facedown on the wrong side of the fabric; position them without space in between (see Diagram 2, template B). Using sharp scissors or a rotary cutter and ruler, cut precisely on the drawn (cutting) lines.

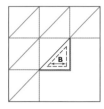

Diagram 2

Templates for Angled Pieces

When two patchwork pieces come together and form an angled opening, a third piece must be set into this angle. This happens frequently when using diamond shapes.

For a design that requires setting in, a pinhole or window template makes it easy to mark the fabric with each shape's exact sewing and cutting lines and the exact point of each corner on the sewing line. By matching the corners of adjacent pieces, you'll be able to sew them together easily and accurately.

To make a pinhole template, lay template plastic over a pattern piece. Trace both the cutting and sewing lines onto the plastic. Carefully cut out the template on the cutting line. Using a sewing-machine needle or any large needle, make a hole in the template at each corner on the sewing line (matching points). The holes must be large enough for a pencil point or other fabric marker to poke through.

Trace Angled Pieces

To mark fabric using a pinhole template, lay it facedown on the wrong side of the fabric and trace. Using a pencil, mark dots on the fabric through the holes in the template to create matching points, then cut out the fabric piece on the drawn line.

To mark fabric using a window template, lay it facedown on the wrong side of the fabric (see Diagram 3). With a marking tool, mark the cutting line, sewing line, and each corner on the sewing line (matching points). Cut out the fabric piece on the cutting lines, making sure all pieces have sewing lines and matching points marked.

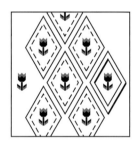

Diagram 3

PIECING

Patchwork piecing consists of sewing fabric pieces together in a specific pattern.

Hand Piecing

In hand piecing, seams are sewn only on the marked sewing lines; the seam allowances remain unstitched. Begin by matching the edges of two pieces with the fabrics' right sides together. Sewing lines should be marked on the wrong side of both pieces. Push a pin through both fabric layers at each corner (see Diagram 1). Secure the pins perpendicular to the sewing line. Insert more pins between the corners.

Insert a needle through both fabrics at the seam-line corner. Make one or two backstitches atop the first stitch to secure the thread. Weave the needle in and out of the fabric along the seam line, taking four to six tiny stitches at a time before you pull the thread taut (see Diagram 2). Remove the pins as you sew. Turn the work over occasionally to see that the stitching follows the marked sewing line on the other side.

Sew eight to 10 stitches per inch along the seam line. At the end of the seam, remove the last pin and make the ending stitch through the hole left

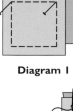

Diagram 1

Diagram 2

Diagram 3

by the corner pin. Backstitch over the last stitch and end the seam with a loop knot (see Diagram 3).

To join rows of patchwork by hand, hold the sewn pieces with right sides together and seams matched. Insert pins at the corners of the matching pieces. Add additional pins as necessary, securing each pin perpendicular to the sewing line (see Diagram 4).

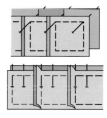

Diagram 4

Stitch the joining seam as before, but do not sew across the seam allowances that join the patches. At each seam allowance, make a backstitch or loop knot, then slide the needle through the seam allowance (see Diagram 5). Knot or backstitch again to give the intersection strength, then sew the remainder of the seam. Press each seam as it is completed.

Diagram 5

Machine piecing depends on sewing an exact ¼" seam allowance. Some machines have a presser foot that is the proper width, or a ¼" foot is

available. To check the width of a machine's presser foot, sew a sample seam with the raw fabric edges aligned with the right edge of the presser foot; measure the resultant seam allowance using graph paper with a ¼" grid.

Using two different thread colors—one on top of the machine and one in the bobbin—can help you to better match your thread color to your fabrics. If your quilt has many fabrics, use a neutral color, such as gray or beige, for both the top and bobbin threads throughout the quilt.

Press for Success

In quilting, almost every seam needs to be pressed before the piece is sewn to another, so keep your iron and ironing board near your sewing area. It's important to remember to press with an up and down motion. Moving the iron around on the fabric can distort seams, especially those sewn on the bias.

Project instructions in this book generally tell you in what direction to press each seam. When in doubt, press both seam allowances toward the darker fabric. When joining rows of blocks, alternate the direction the seam allowances are pressed to ensure flat corners.

Setting in Pieces

The key to sewing angled pieces together is aligning marked matching points carefully. Whether you're stitching by machine or hand, start and stop sewing precisely at the matching points (see the dots in Diagram 6, top) and backstitch to secure the ends of the seams. This prepares the angle for the next piece to be set in.

Join two diamond pieces, sewing between matching points to make an angled unit (see Diagram 6).

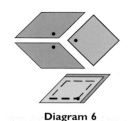

Diagram 6

Follow the specific instructions for either machine or hand piecing to complete the set-in seam.

MACHINE PIECING

With right sides together, pin one piece of the angled unit to one edge of the square (see Diagram 7). Match the seam's matching points by pushing a pin through both fabric layers to check the alignment. Machine-stitch the seam between the matching points. Backstitch to secure the ends of the seam; do not stitch into the ¼" seam allowance. Remove the unit from the sewing machine.

Bring the adjacent edge of the angled unit up and align it with the next edge of the square (see Diagram 8). Insert a pin in each corner to align matching points, then pin the remainder of the seam. Machine-stitch between matching points as before. Press the seam allowances of the set-in piece away from it.

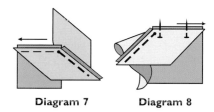

Diagram 7   **Diagram 8**

HAND PIECING

Pin one piece of the angled unit to one edge of the square with right sides together (see Diagram 9). Use pins to align matching points at the corners.

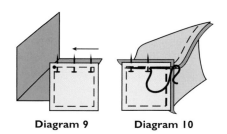

Diagram 9   **Diagram 10**

Hand-sew the seam from the open end of the angle into the corner. Remove pins as you sew between matching points. Backstitch at the corner to secure stitches. Do not sew into the ¼" seam allowance and do not cut your thread.

continued

Bring the adjacent edge of the square up and align it with the other edge of the angled unit. Insert a pin in each corner to align matching points, then pin the remainder of the seam (see Diagram 10 on *page 155*). Continuing the thread from the previous seam, hand-sew the seam from the corner to the open end of the angle, removing pins as you sew. Press the seam allowances of the set-in piece away from it.

Mitered Border Corners

A border surrounds the piecework of many quilts. Angled, mitered corners add to a border's framed effect.

To add a border with mitered corners, first pin a border strip to a quilt top edge, matching the center of the strip and the center of the quilt top edge. Allow excess border fabric to extend beyond the edges. Sew together, beginning and ending the seam ¼" from the quilt top corners (see Diagram 11). Repeat with the remaining border strips. Press the seam allowances toward the border strips.

Overlap the border strips at each corner (see Diagram 12). Align the edge of a 90° right triangle with the raw edge of a top border strip so the long edge of the triangle intersects the seam in the corner. With a pencil, draw along the edge of the triangle from the border seam out to the raw edge. Place the bottom border strip on top and repeat the marking process.

With the right sides of adjacent border strips together, match the marked seam lines and pin (see Diagram 13).

Beginning with a backstitch at the inside corner, stitch exactly on the marked lines to the outside edges of the border strips. Check the right side of the corner to see that it lies flat. Then trim the excess fabric, leaving a ¼" seam allowance. Press the seam open. Mark and sew the remaining corners in this manner.

Diagram 11

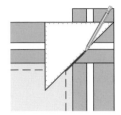

Diagram 12

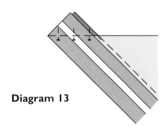

Diagram 13

APPLIQUÉ

With appliqué, you create a picture by stitching fabric shapes atop a fabric foundation.

Start Simple

We encourage beginners to select an appliqué design with straight lines and gentle curves. Learning to make sharp points and tiny stitches takes practice.

In the following instructions, we've used a stemmed flower motif as the appliqué example.

Baste the Seam Allowances

Begin by turning under the ³⁄₁₆" seam allowances on the appliqué pieces; press. Some quilters like to thread-baste the folded edges to ensure proper placement. Edges that will be covered by other pieces don't need to be turned under.

For sharp points on tips, first trim the seam allowance to within ⅛" of the stitching line (see Photo 1, *opposite*), tapering the sides gradually to ³⁄₁₆". Fold under the seam allowance remaining on the tips. Then turn the seam allowances under on both sides of the tips. The side seam allowances will overlap slightly at the tips, forming sharp points.

Baste the folded edges in place (see Photo 2, *opposite*). The turned seam allowances may form little pleats on the back side that you also should baste in place. Remove the basting stitches after the shapes have been appliquéd to the foundation.

Make Bias Stems

In order to curve gracefully, appliqué stems are cut on the bias. The strips for stems can be prepared in two ways. You can fold and press the strip in thirds as shown in Photo 3, *opposite*. Or you can fold the bias strip in half lengthwise with the wrong side inside; press. Stitch ¼" in from the raw edges to keep them aligned. Fold the strip in half again, hiding the raw edges behind the first folded edge; press.

Position and Stitch

Pin the prepared appliqué pieces in place on the foundation (see Photo 4, *opposite*) using the position markings or referring to the block assembly diagram. If your pattern suggests it, mark the position for each piece on the foundation before you begin. Overlap the flowers and stems as indicated.

Using thread in colors that match the fabrics, sew each stem and blossom onto the foundation with small slip stitches as shown in Photo 5. (For photographic purposes, thread color does not match fabric color.)

Catch only a few threads of the stem or flower fold with each stitch. Pull the stitches taut, but not so tight that they pucker the fabric. You can use the needle's point to manipulate the appliqué edges as needed. Take an extra slip stitch at the point of a petal to secure it to the foundation.

You can use hand-quilting needles for appliqué stitching, but some quilters prefer a longer milliner's or straw needle. The extra needle length aids in tucking fabric under before taking slip stitches.

If the foundation fabric shows through the appliqué fabrics, cut away the foundation fabric. Trimming the foundation fabric also reduces the bulk of multiple layers when quilting later. Carefully trim the underlying fabric to within ¼" of the appliqué stitches (see Photo 6) and avoid cutting the appliqué fabrics.

Fusible Appliqué

For quick-finish appliqué, use paper-backed lightweight fusible web and iron the shapes onto the foundation and add decorative stitching to the edges. This product consists of two layers, a fusible webbing lightly bonded to paper that peels off. The webbing adds a slight stiffness to the back of the appliqué pieces.

When you purchase this product, read the directions on the bolt end or packaging to make sure you're buying the right kind for your project. Some brands are specifically engineered to

bond fabrics with no sewing at all. If you try to stitch fabric after it has bonded with one of these products, you may encounter difficulty. Some paper-backed fusible products are made exclusively for sewn edges; others work with or without stitching.

If you buy paper-backed fusible web from a bolt, be sure fusing instructions are included because the iron temperature and timing varies by brand. This information is usually on the paper backing.

With any of these products, the general procedure is to trace the patterns wrong side up onto the

paper side of the fusible web. Then place the fusible-web pieces on the wrong side of the appliqué fabrics, paper side up, and use an iron to fuse the layers together. Then cut out the fabric shapes, peel off the paper, turn the fabrics right side up, and fuse them to the foundation fabric.

You also can fuse the fusible web and fabric together before tracing. You'll still need to trace templates wrong side up on the paper backing.

If you've used a no-sew fusible web, your appliqué is done. If not, finish the edges with hand or machine stitching.

CUTTING BIAS STRIPS

Strips for curved appliqué pattern pieces, such as meandering vines, and for binding curved edges should be cut on the bias, which runs at a 45° angle to the selvage of a woven fabric and has the most give or stretch.

To cut bias strips, begin with a fabric square or rectangle. Use a large

acrylic ruler to square up the left edge of the fabric. Then make a cut at a 45° angle to the left edge (see Bias Strip Diagram). Handle the diagonal edges carefully to avoid distorting the bias. To cut a strip, measure the desired width parallel to the 45° cut edge; cut. Continue cutting enough strips to total the length needed.

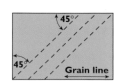

Bias Strip Diagram

COVERED CORDING

Finish pillows and quilts with easy, tailored cording.

Covered cording is made by sewing a bias-cut fabric strip around a length of cording. The width of the bias strip varies according to the diameter of your cording. Refer to the specific project instructions for those measurements. Regardless, the method used to cover the cording is the same.

With the wrong side inside, fold under 1½" at one end of the bias strip. With the wrong side inside, fold the strip in half lengthwise to make the cording cover. Insert the cording next to the folded edge, placing a cording end 1" from the cording cover folded end. Using a machine cording foot, sew through both fabric layers right next to the cording (see Diagram 1).

When attaching the cording to your project, begin stitching 1½" from the covered cording's folded end. Round the corners slightly, making sure the corner curves match. As you stitch each corner, gently ease the covered cording into place (see Diagram 2).

After going around the entire edge of the project, cut the end of the cording so that it will fit snugly into the folded opening at the beginning (see Diagram 3). The ends of the cording should abut inside the covering. Stitch the ends in place to secure (see Diagram 4).

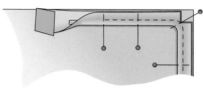

Diagram 2

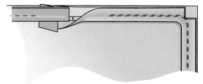

Diagram 3

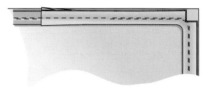

Diagram 4

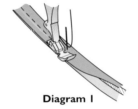

Diagram 1

HANGING SLEEVES

When you want a favorite quilt to become wall art,

hang it with care to avoid sagging, tearing, and wavy edges.

Quilts make wonderful pieces of wall art. When treated as museum pieces and hung properly, they won't deteriorate. Let size be your guide when determining how to hang your quilt.

Hang smaller quilts, a 25" square or less, with purchased clips, sewn-on tabs, or pins applied to the corners. Larger quilts require a hanging sleeve attached to the back. It may take a few minutes more to sew on a sleeve, but the effort preserves your hours of work with less distortion and damage.

Make a Hanging Sleeve

1. Measure the quilt's top edge.

2. Cut a 6"- to 10"-wide strip of prewashed fabric 2" longer than the quilt's top edge. For example, if the top edge is 40", cut a 6×42" strip. A 6"-wide strip is sufficient for a dowel or drapery rod. If you're using something bigger in diameter, cut a wider fabric strip. If you're sending your quilt to be displayed at a quilt show, adjust your

Diagram 1

Diagram 2

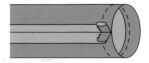

Diagram 3

measurements to accommodate the show's requirements.

3. Fold under 1½" on both ends of the fabric strip. Sew ¼" from the raw edges (see Diagram 1).

4. Fold the fabric strip in half lengthwise with the wrong side inside; pin. Stitch together the long edges with a ¼" seam allowance (see Diagram 2) to make the sleeve. Press

the seam allowance open and center the seam in the middle of the sleeve (see Diagram 3).

5. Center the sleeve on the quilt back about 1" below the binding with the seam facing the back (see Diagram 4). Slip-stitch the sleeve to the quilt along both long edges and the portions of the short edges that touch the back, stitching through the back and batting.

Diagram 4

6. Slide a wooden dowel or slender piece of wood that is 1" longer than the finished sleeve into the sleeve and hang as desired.

FINISHING

The final step in quiltmaking is to bind the edges.

Layering

Cut and piece the backing fabric to measure at least 3" bigger on all sides than the quilt top. Press all seam allowances open. With wrong sides together, layer the quilt top and backing fabric with the batting in between; baste. Quilt as desired.

Binding

The binding for most quilts is cut on the straight grain of the fabric. If your quilt has curved edges, cut the strips on the bias (see *page 157*). The cutting instructions for projects in this book specify the number of binding strips or a total length needed to finish the quilt. The instructions also specify enough width for a French-fold, or double-layer, binding because it's easier to apply and adds durability.

Join the strips with diagonal seams to make one continuous binding strip

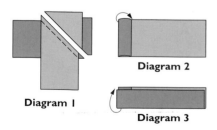

Diagram 1

Diagram 2

Diagram 3

(see Diagram 1). Trim the excess fabric, leaving ¼" seam allowances. Press the seam allowances open. Then, with the wrong sides together, fold under 1" at one end of the binding strip (see Diagram 2); press. Fold the strip in half lengthwise (see Diagram 3); press.

Beginning in the center of one side, place the binding strip against the right side of the quilt top, aligning the binding strip's raw edges with the quilt top's raw edge (see Diagram 4). Beginning 1½" from the folded edge, sew through all layers, stopping ¼" from the corner. Backstitch, then clip the threads. Remove the quilt from under the sewing-machine presser foot.

Fold the binding strip upward (see Diagram 5), creating a diagonal fold, and finger-press.

Holding the diagonal fold in place with your finger, bring the binding strip down in line with the next edge, making a horizontal fold that aligns with the first edge of the quilt (see Diagram 6).

Start sewing again at the top of the horizontal fold, stitching through all layers. Sew around the quilt, turning each corner in the same manner.

When you return to the starting point, lap the binding strip inside the beginning fold (see Diagram 7).

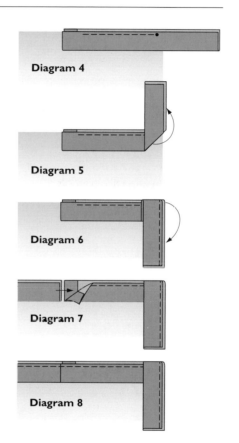

Diagram 4

Diagram 5

Diagram 6

Diagram 7

Diagram 8

Finish sewing to the starting point (see Diagram 8). Trim the batting and backing fabric even with the quilt top edges.

Turn the binding over the edge of the quilt to the back. Hand-stitch the binding to the backing fabric, making sure to cover any machine stitching.

To make mitered corners on the back, hand-stitch the binding up to a corner; fold a miter in the binding. Take a stitch or two in the fold to secure it. Then stitch the binding in place up to the next corner. Finish each corner in the same manner.

CREDITS

Quilt Designers

Leslie Beck and her staff at Fiber Mosaics
Twilight
When Leslie Beck and staff members at Fiber Mosaics in Kennewick, Washington, explore a design idea, they consider the variety of ways it can be used.

Cindy Blackberg and Mary Sorensen
Gathering Baskets
Cindy Blackberg, *far left,* of Sorrento, Florida, and Mary Sorensen of Longwood, Florida, enjoy team-teaching hand piecing and needle-turn appliqué.

Lynn Dash
Cottage Dreams
Lynn Dash of Grafton, Virginia, enjoys both hand quilting and machine quilting.

Claudia Fix and Dana Barnett
Sisters' Starberries
Sisters Dana Barnett, *far left,* and Claudia Fix of Wray, Colorado, often collaborate on quilt designs, incorporating Claudia's appliqué skills and Dana's favorite fabrics.

Peggy Kotek
Sweet Lullabies
Designer and teacher Peggy Kotek of Madison Lake, Minnesota, enjoys bringing new life to traditional quilt patterns.

Ann Lage
Abby's Wish
Quilt designer Ann Lage of Omaha, Nebraska, created and named this quilt in honor of her granddaughter, Abby.

Carla Malkiewicz
Brilliant Trip Around the World
Quilt shop teacher Carla Malkiewicz of Conroe, Texas, enjoys working with her patchwork specialty—bargello.

Marti Michell
Texas Stars
Marti Michell of Marietta, Georgia, teaches quiltmaking, writes books, designs patterns, and develops specialty tools for quilters.

Jan Ragaller
Tiger Lily
Jan Ragaller of Rockford, Illinois, publishes her quilt designs under the Penny Candy Press imprint.

Jill Reber
Heaven's Stairway
Jill Reber of Granger, Iowa, collaborated with her husband, Jim, to create Master Piece rulers and patterns for quilters.

Peggy Waltman
Serendipity
From her home in Sandy, Utah, quilt designer and author Peggy Waltman of Hopskotch Quilting Company quilts nearly six hours a day.

Darlene Zimmerman
Baskets of Stars
Darlene Zimmerman of Fairfax, Minnesota, is a designer of quilts, fabrics, and quilting tools, as well as an author and teacher.

Laura Boehnke
Quilt Tester
With a keen color sense and astute use of fabrics, quilt tester Laura Boehnke gives each project an entirely different look when she verifies the pattern, a job she's been doing for *American Patchwork & Quilting®* magazine since its inception.

Project Quilters and Finishers

Jacalyn Bell
Laura Boehnke
Janet Brandt
Dorothy Faidley
Karen Gilson
Kate Hardy
Rosann Kermes
Becky Larson
Jill Abeloe Mead
Mabeth Oxenreider
Mary Pepper
Janet Pittman
Janelle Swenson
Sue Urich
Kathleen Williams
Molly Zearing
Darlene Zimmerman

Materials Suppliers

Benartex
Chanteclaire
Hoffman Fabrics
Fairfield Processing Corp.
Kings Road
Moda
Northcott Silk
P&B Textiles
Red Rooster Fabrics
RJR Fabrics
Robert Kaufman Fine Fabrics
Sulky Threads
Timeless Treasures

Photographers

Craig Anderson: pages 31, 33, 44, 47, 54, 75, 82, 102, 104, 105, 118, 138, 141, and 149
Marcia Cameron: pages 10, 11, 20, 22, 45, 52, 72, 84, 85, 93, 109, 128, 134, and 138
Scott Little: pages 30 and 83
Perry Struse: pages 9, 13, 15, 17, 21, 23, 25, 32, 37, 43, 46, 48, 53, 55, 56, 61, 63, 66, 71, 74, 77, 81, 86, 91, 92, 96, 101, 103, 107, 111, 112, 114, 119, 124, 129, 131, 133, 139, 140, 143, 147, and 148
Steve Struse: pages 18, 28, 38, 59, 69, 90, 99, 108, and 116